O9-BTJ-772

WI

LEVANA COOKS DAIRY-FREE!

LEVANA COOKS DAIRY-FREE!

Natural and Delicious Recipes for Your Favorite "Forbidden" Foods

Lévana Kirschenbaum

Photos by
Menachem Adelman and Meir Pliskin

Skyhorse Publishing

www.skyhorsepublishing.com

Library of Congress Cataloging-in-Publication Data

Kirschenbaum, Lévana.
Levana cooks dairy-free!: Natural and Delicious Recipes for Your Favorite "Forbidden" Foods/ Lévana Kirschenbaum; photos by Menachem Adelman and Meir Pliskin.

   p. cm.

ISBN-13: 978-1-60239-083-6 (alk. paper)
ISBN-10: 1-60239-083-5 (alk. paper)

1. Milk-free diet—Recipes. 2. Dairy substitutes. I. Title.

RM234.5.K57 2007
641.5'63—dc22

                        2007020062

10 9 8 7 6 5 4 3 2 1

Printed in China

ALSO BY LÉVANA KIRSCHENBAUM

Levana's Table: Kosher Cooking for Everyone
In Short Order: Book-Demo DVD Set

To
Maurice, Maimon, Ruthie,
Mousia, Sarah Esther, Yakov, Elisheva,
Bella, and Meir

CONTENTS

ACKNOWLEDGMENTS

Almost everyone who sampled the recipes in this book asked me the same naïve question: Is there ever a time I try putting a dish together and "it just doesn't work"? So this must be the hallmark of a good cook and food chemist, that the end result is so good no trace remains of all the trial and error period. I can get pretty dogged, which is an asset I have rarely needed more than for this project: I worked with improbable ingredients and by all accounts ended up with fabulous results. I braved all the skeptical smirks that preceded the tasting of my dairy-free crème caramel or cheesecake or lasagna and was amply rewarded with countless converts.

Special thanks to my friend Jonathan Seliger, who got the ball rolling; to my agent and neighbor Jennifer Lyons; to my talented and efficient editor Abigail Gehring; to all the people I have enslaved during the writing of the book and the photo shoot: Barbara Chazan, Fabia Preminger, my daughter Bella, my daughter-in-law Elisheva, my talented son-in-law Meir Pliskin, Menachem and Leah Adelman; to my friends Georganne Garfinkel, Karen Wallman, and Larisa Gelfman; to the owners of the gift store "Impressions," several of whose gorgeous dishes grace our pictures; to my great family of students who have always made my work a pleasure.

INTRODUCTION

About a year ago, the producers of a popular New York television station got wind of my wizardry with non-dairy cooking and invited me to appear on their morning show. They wanted to do a blind tasting in which three of my dairy-free desserts would face off against their dairy counterparts. Talk about a triumph: The results of that presentation were astounding. The tasters found that one of the desserts (an apricot mousse) tasted virtually identical made either way, while the other two (a cheesecake and a chocolate hazelnut mousse torte) were more delicious made without cow's milk, cheese, or butter.

I believe that anyone, even the novice cook, can prepare practically any dish without dairy products and come up with something delicious. I can, and I know that most other people can, too. But too many cooks still believe that a meal that is not traditionally prepared with milk or butter can never be as good. This book proves just how wrong this assumption is—and the feeling of liberation it will give cooks will be wonderful. How do I know this? Because over the past twenty-nine years, as a cooking teacher, cookbook author, and owner of a bakery, a kosher catering business, and Levana Restaurant in Manhattan, I've learned a thing or two about dairy-free cooking. I had to because, like fifty million other Americans, I am mostly lactose-intolerant. And like many of my students, my customers, and an estimated twenty-five percent of American Jews, I observe the kosher dietary laws. This means that it is verboten to mix meat and dairy in the same meal. In one fell swoop, I am recasting vast numbers of dishes and many delicious desserts that had been previously barred from many meals. Observing kosher requirements means I make sure not to use any of the products that purport to be dairy-free yet still contain traces of whey, butter, and other banned ingredients, which suits the lactose-intolerant community as well.

The truth is we all love dairy products, but that love is too often unrequited by our religion, our bodies, or both. My family, friends, customers, and students are always clamoring for alternatives that are free of the offending ingredients. Although I give cooking demonstrations on every imaginable culinary topic, I get the most requests for dairy-free cooking.

It is important to note that I do not use simple substitutions. For years, I have experimented and played with ingredients that most cooks have ignored, such as soy and other non-dairy (rice, oat, grain, almond, coconut) milks, soy cream cheese and sour cream, nut butters, flours, and alternative sweeteners. For example, many kosher cooks feel they must use non-dairy creamer instead of milk products, or margarine instead of butter, and just accept the compromised flavor. I don't think that is tolerable at all, and so I have a different approach—one that uses only natural products. My number one theme is to demolish the notion that someone cooking with restrictions must rely on substitute ingredients that are "sort of" the same. No. Every ingredient I use stands on its own merits as a delicious, natural, wholesome addition to a recipe. Lest you misconstrue the purpose of this book, I hasten to add that it doesn't provide an excuse for having a field day emulating rich junk foods such as cheeseburgers, salami-and-cheese sandwiches, pepperoni-and-cheese pizza, and goodness knows what other calamities. I have no complicity whatsoever with the fast-food crowd. My repertoire is simple yet politically correct through and through, from a nutritional as well as a kosher standpoint. So, I invite you to enjoy my dairy-free renditions of your favorite treats without fear or guilt!

Rather than give you a long, tedious list of sources for non-dairy ingredients, I am referring you to a wonderful book compiled by Alisa Fleming, who also started a major non-dairy site, www.godairyfree. com. The book is called *Dairy-Free Made Easy*. Since we share a passion for good and healthy non-dairy cuisine, it was only natural that our paths would cross. There is no consideration Alisa hasn't addressed. Each ingredient's features are extensively itemized wherever applicable: whether it is organic, kosher, vegan, gluten-free, soy-free, etc. … in short, everything you need to know: It's all in there!

LEVANA COOKS DAIRY-FREE!

Breakfast and Brunch Dishes

- 🍽 Smoothies
- 🍽 Corn bread
- 🍽 Apple nut muffins
- 🍽 Blueberry scones
- 🍽 Babka
- 🍽 Crepes
- 🍽 Red pepper and zucchini frittata
- 🍽 Salmon tomato quiche
- 🍽 Salmon mousse
- 🍽 Eggs benedict
- 🍽 Marinated tomato and tofu salad
- 🍽 Fruited noodle pudding

SMOOTHIES

Smoothies are a wonderful way to sneak nutrients into a diet, and you can make endless variations. My trick is, don't use ice, but use frozen fruit. In one fell swoop, you get the fruit and the ice and so much more flavor. Plus, frozen fruit often tastes better than fresh because they are picked at their ripest and sweetest, and they require no cleaning or rinsing. Bananas got too ripe? Just stick them in the freezer, the riper the better, and when you need them, run them under warm water—the peels will come right off. Make a large smoothie batch and save the rest for later in the blender. If the mixture separates, give the blender a few turns again. If you are thinking of offering grownup brunch drinks, simply add half a cup of vodka to the mix!

Berry Smoothies

Makes 5 cups

1 cup cranberry or pomegranate juice
1 cup silken tofu, soy or other non-dairy milk (rice, grain, oat, almond)
2 cups frozen berries (strawberries, blueberries, raspberries, blackberries, alone or in any combination)
2 tablespoons honey, maple syrup, or cranberry or pomegranate concentrate (health food stores), only if you like it sweeter

Mix all ingredients in the blender a full minute at high speed until smooth and frothy.

Green Smoothies

Try your best to stick some of the fruit in the freezer for an hour before blending. No need to have all of these fruit on hand; even a combination of two in larger amounts will be delicious.

Makes 5 cups

1 cup green grapes
1 large pear or green apple, unpeeled, cut in chunks
3 ripe kiwis, peeled
1 cup chunks honeydew melon
1 cup white grape juice or natural apple cider
A few leaves fresh mint, if you have them on hand

Mix all ingredients in the blender a full minute at high speed until smooth and frothy.

Chocolate Almond Date Smoothie

Consider this a whole meal. Nutritious and fabulous! This is the only smoothie I use ice with, to chill the heated mixture.

Makes 5 cups

1/2 cup whole almonds

1 cup pitted dates, packed
1/3 cup cocoa powder
1 cup boiling water
1 cup silken tofu, soy or any other non-dairy milk (rice, grain, oat, almond)
A dozen ice cubes

Place the almonds, dates, cocoa, and water in the blender. Cover and let the mixture rest, unblended, 5 to 10 minutes. Add the tofu or milk and ice and blend a full minute at high speed until thick and frothy.

Tropical Smoothies

If you decide to get a little naughtier with this smoothie, add 1/2 cup dark rum. You know how the saying goes: If you can't go to the tropics…

Makes about 6 cups

2 cups canned unsweetened pineapple chunks, juice and all
1 cup coconut milk
3 cups cubed mango, papaya, or peaches: try your best for frozen
1 banana: try your best for frozen

Mix all ingredients in the blender a full minute at high speed until smooth and frothy.

Beet Smoothies

Here is your chance to eat your beets! Who knew they were so delicious? I did; we grew up eating them every day. In America, they are sometimes treated like a poor stepchild of the vegetable family. I think it is time to adopt them wholeheartedly. They are so good for you.

Makes 1 serving

1 small can beets, juice and all
1 cup tofu or unflavored soy yogurt

Mix all ingredients in the blender a full minute at high speed until smooth and frothy.

CORN BREAD

Corn bread is one of those comfort foods that is welcome anytime—alone, with your favorite spread, or as an edible scoop for chili. Because it is a quick bread, no need to premeditate any bread kneading or rising. It is ready at the drop of a hat. The trick for a great corn bread is to stick a heavy skillet in a hot oven while you prepare the batter, so the bread gets a great head start in the very first few seconds of baking.

Makes 6 servings

1 1/4 cups soy milk
2 tablespoons lemon juice
1 egg
2 tablespoons vegetable oil

1 1/4 cups medium corn meal
3/4 cup all-purpose flour (whole wheat pastry flour or spelt flour O.K.)
1 teaspoon baking powder
1 teaspoon baking soda
1/2 teaspoon salt
3 tablespoons sugar

Preheat the oven to 400°F.

Grease a round 9-inch heavy skillet, and put it in the oven while you mix the bread. Mix the soy milk and lemon juice in a bowl. The mixture will curdle. Add the egg and the oil, and mix. In another bowl, mix the corn meal, flour, baking powder, baking soda, salt, and sugar thoroughly with a spoon. Pour the egg mixture into the flour mixture and mix until just combined. Immediately pour the mixture into the hot pan. Bake about 20 minutes, or until the top is cracked and golden. Serve warm or at room temperature.

Corn Muffins

Makes a dozen medium muffins

Grease a muffin pan and place in the oven while you prepare the batter. Proceed as above.

Tex-Mex Corn Bread

To the initial batter, add 4 sprigs minced dill or cilantro, 1 small grated onion, 1 minced jalapeno pepper, 2 teaspoons cumin. Optional: Add 1 cup frozen chopped corn kernels and 1/2 cup grated VeganRella cheese. Proceed as above.

BUTTERMILK

For a delicious corn bread and many other treats, we need the tangy flavor and clotted texture of buttermilk, which yields wonderfully moist and tender results. I found a perfect buttermilk substitute by mixing 1 cup of soy milk (alas, other non-dairy milks won't work; only soy milk does the trick) with 1 tablespoon lemon juice or vinegar. In a matter of seconds, the mixture will "curdle" and be ready to use exactly as buttermilk.

APPLE NUT MUFFINS

This recipe gives you an unlimited opportunity to play with sweeteners, fruits, nuts, and flours, making endless permutations and creating as large and nutritious a selection of muffins as you will ever need. Eating this kind of muffin is actually a good kind of weakness, so don't worry if your kids clamor for more!

Makes 12 to 15 medium muffins

Vegetable spray
1 cup soy milk or any other non-dairy milk (rice, oat, almond, grain)
2 large eggs
1/3 cup vegetable oil
1 cup dark brown sugar
2 Granny Smith apples, peeled, cored, and grated coarsely in a food processor

2 cup old-fashioned oats
3 cups all-purpose flour
1 1/2 teaspoons baking powder
1 teaspoon baking soda
1/2 teaspoon salt
1/2 cup raisins
1/2 cup chopped walnuts or pecans
1 teaspoon cinnamon

Preheat the oven to 375 °F. Spray a 12-cup muffin tin with vegetable spray.

Combine the milk, eggs, oil, brown sugar, and apples, and mix thoroughly. In another bowl, combine the oats, flour, baking powder, baking soda, salt, raisins, and nuts. Add the dry mixture to the milk mixture. Combine gently but thoroughly with a spoon, taking care not to over-mix, which would toughen the batter.

Pour the batter into the prepared muffin pans. Bake for about 30 minutes, or until a toothpick inserted in the center comes out clean.

ALL SUBSTITUTIONS IN EQUAL AMOUNTS

- For the all-purpose flour, substitute whole wheat pastry or spelt flour.
- For the oil, substitute coconut or flax oil, tehina, or any natural nut butter.
- For raisins, substitute dried cranberries or other chopped dry fruit (prunes, apricots, dates, figs, etc.).
- For grated apple, substitute grated carrot or zucchini.
- For walnuts, substitute almonds or pumpkin, flax, sesame, or sunflower seeds.
- For brown sugar, substitute sucanat, rapadura, date sugar, or malt sugar (health food stores).
- For cinnamon, substitute ground ginger, cardamom, or all spice.
- For rolled oats, substitute barley, quinoa, spelt, soy, or other flakes.
- If you are egg-restricted, see box on eggs (p.13).

TO MAKE A LOAF

This batter makes a delicious bread loaf. Bake in a greased loaf pan in a preheated 350 °F oven, 45 minutes to one hour, or until a knife inserted in the center of the loaf comes out clean.

BLUEBERRY SCONES

I adore blueberries and cash in on their great abundance all summer long, eating them out of hand until I get blue in the face (excuse the pun), or using them in cakes, tarts, cobblers, vinegars, you name it. I can't bear to see them go into hibernation all those long berry-less months! In this recipe, dry blueberries are quite an acceptable substitute, and they are available year round (expensive, but a little goes a long way). Do not substitute frozen in this or any recipe calling for blueberries other than smoothies, fruit sauces, and cobblers, because they make your batter a disagreeable blue mess, as if you forgot to take a pen out from a pocket before loading your washing machine, as once happened to me. (Oy, don't try that!)

These scones are packed with flavor and take less than five minutes to assemble, making them ideal for brunch.

Makes about 2 dozen scones

3 cups all-purpose flour (or spelt flour)
1/4 cup sugar, or up to 1/3 cup, if you like them a little sweeter
1/3 cup natural non-hydrogenated margarine (health-food stores)
4 teaspoons baking powder
1 teaspoon baking soda
1/4 teaspoon salt
1 tablespoon grated orange zest
1 cup plain soy yogurt
1 egg, lightly beaten
1 1/4 cups fresh blueberries, or 3/4 cup dried blueberries

Preheat the oven to 400 °F.

Mix the flour, sugar, and margarine with a pastry blender or two knives, until the mixture resembles coarse meal. Add the baking powder, baking soda, salt, and orange zest and mix. Add the yogurt and egg and mix until just combined. Add the blueberries and mix very gently so as not to extract their moisture (this won't apply if you are using dry blueberries).

Roll out the dough on a very lightly floured board to 1/2-inch thickness. Cut out with a 2-inch cookie cutter or the rim of a glass. Transfer to a cookie sheet lined with foil. Bake about 15 minutes, or until lightly colored.

> ## MARGARINE
>
> Now that there are so many new brands of natural, non-hydrogenated margarines available, I don't have the qualms I used to have about using margarine. Only, please read the labels and be sure you are picking the non-hydrogenated type. They rarely come in sticks, mostly in tubs, and even though they look less firm than their hydrogenated counterparts, they do the job. Don't use the "light" ones that use water in the mix—they don't work for baking.

BABKA

This yeasted pastry bears an affectionate name in every language (brioche, kugelhopf, kokosh, etc.) and varies only slightly in preparation from one culture to another, but whatever you call it, it is always fabulous, even without the butter and the milk. Do not hesitate to double, even triple, the recipe, as it freezes very well.

Makes 8 servings

1 envelope dry yeast
1/4 cup warm water
1/3 cup sugar or honey

2 3/4 cups flour, plus a little more if needed
1/4 cup oil, plus a little more for brushing
1/2 cup soy or other non-dairy milk (rice, oat, grain, almond)
1 egg
1/3 teaspoon salt

Topping (optional)

1 tablespoon oil
1/4 cup flour
3 tablespoons sugar

Mix the yeast, water, and sugar in a cup and let the mixture stand a minute or two, or until it comes to a bubble. Put all the other ingredients in a mixing bowl. Add the yeast mixture and combine. Transfer to your dough maker and knead 10 minutes, or knead by hand.

Let the dough rise, covered, in a warm draft-free place one hour.

Preheat the oven to 350 °F. On a very lightly floured board or counter, roll out the dough into a thin, 20- by 8-inch rectangle. Brush the whole surface very lightly with oil. Sprinkle or spread the filling on the whole surface (recipes follow). Roll very tightly. Transfer to a greased loaf pan. Mix the topping ingredients, and sprinkle over the babka. (If not using the topping, simply brush with a mixture of egg and water.) Bake 35 to 40 minutes, until golden.

FILLINGS

Chocolate: Melt 2/3 cup very good quality real chocolate chips with 1 tablespoon oil.
Cinnamon-raisin: In a food processor, process until coarsely ground: 1/2 cup golden raisins, 1/3 cup walnuts, 1/4 cup brown sugar, 1–2 teaspoons cinnamon.
Jam: 1 cup good black currant, strawberry, or raspberry preserves thinned with 2–3 tablespoons orange juice.

CREPES

Feather-light, ready in a minute, and so versatile! I play with every kind of flour I find in health food stores and get different and exciting results each time. Any leftover batter will keep a couple days refrigerated; just thin it with a little water or non-dairy milk if it got too thick, and give it a few turns in the blender. At any one seating, my family and I have half a dozen fillings to choose from (see page 14).

Makes a dozen crepes

4 eggs, or 8 egg whites if you are watching your cholesterol intake
2 cups all-purpose flour, or any flour you like
1 1/2 cups cold soy or other non-dairy milk (rice, oat, grain, almond)
1 cup cold water or seltzer
2 tablespoons vegetable oil
Pinch salt

DESSERT CREPES

Add a teaspoon vanilla extract and 2 tablespoons sugar, maple syrup, or honey.

Blend all ingredients in a blender or food processor until smooth. Spray a 9-inch nonstick skillet with cooking spray and let it get really hot. Pour just enough batter to coat the bottom of the pan (use a very small ladle). Start with the center of the skillet and swirl the batter in the pan all around to ensure that the bottom is very thinly and evenly coated. After a few seconds, the edges will start detaching from the bottom of the pan, and the top will look dry. Turn the crepe over and cook for a few more seconds. Transfer to a plate, and repeat with the remaining batter, spraying the pan each time. Use your favorite filling (recipes follow) and roll or fold the crepe over it, or fold and use the filling as a topping. Eat hot.

NON-DAIRY CHEESE

VeganRella brand non-dairy cheese is the best brand I know. It is made with oat and rice flour, so diners limiting their soy intake can enjoy it in any amount. It is 100 percent dairy-free—unlike most other brands of soy cheese, which still contain whey and other dairy traces and therefore defeat the original purpose—and tastes great. No, not as great as a brie or a camembert that makes you think you have just gone to heaven, alas; not delicious enough to eat out of hand, but delicious enough to enjoy when combined with other ingredients. So, thank goodness for small blessings! I served my husband, a cheese lover, these crepes topped with this "cheese," cheddar flavor, and waited until he confirmed it was delicious before I spilled the beans: he didn't believe me!

ALL-FRUIT JAMS

They not only taste fabulous, which is hardly surprising because they pack in so much more fruit than their sugar-based counterparts, but they also have about half the calories. The sweetness comes from the fruit and not sugar. The best brands I know are "Fior di Frutta" and "Brad's Organic Jam," found at health food stores.

FLOUR

While we need to use flour that contains gluten (mostly wheat and spelt) for successful results with breads and cakes, there are quite a few times when we don't: cookies, crepes, dredging, sauces, etc… This is great news for the vast number of gluten-intolerant diners, or even just those who, like me, experiment with the whole gamut of grains. I encourage you to experiment with absolutely every kind of flour you find in health food stores: whole wheat pastry, millet, barley, oat, quinoa, teff, buckwheat, rice, to name just a few. You will obtain a deliciously different flavor each time—the texture never suffers and the nutrition boost is priceless.

EGGS

If you are restricting your egg intake, substitute the following mixture for each egg: 1 tablespoon flax meal and 3 tablespoons water, left to sit a minute or two. While it doesn't work very well for cakes or omelets, it does the trick for cookies and crepes. It's perfect for a great many treats I prepare for my granddaughter, who is allergic to eggs and gets often frustrated at the sight of her classmates and cousins who are eating pancakes and cookies with such gusto!

FILLINGS FOR CREPES

Creamed Spinach Filling

2 tablespoons olive oil
1 small onion, minced
2 tablespoons flour
1 1/2 cups soy or other non-dairy milk (rice, grain, oat, almond)
1 10-ounce box frozen chopped spinach, thawed and squeezed dry
Salt and pepper to taste
1 teaspoon dry basil.
Pinch nutmeg

Heat the oil in a pan. Add the onion and sauté until translucent. Lower the heat and add the flour. Cook two minutes, whisking, until the flour gets a light brown color. Add the milk in a very slow stream, whisking constantly. The mixture will get thick and creamy. It will only take a minute. Add the spinach and remaining seasonings and cook 1 more minute.

Chicken Filling

Substitute 2 cups cooked diced chicken for the spinach.

Mushroom Filling

Substitute 2 cups sautéed mushrooms for the spinach.

Cheese Filling

Substitute 1 cup grated VeganRella brand cheese for the spinach (or no filling: simply grate some on your finished crepe).

Herb Filling

Add your favorite herbs and spices (chives, dill, oregano, garlic, etc.) directly to the batter.

Smoked Salmon or Caviar Filling

Fold the crepe in four, top with a dollop of Tofutti brand sour cream and a dollop of good brand caviar or a thin slice of smoked salmon.

Jam Filling

Spread with a good brand, preferably fruit-sweetened jam.

Fruit Filling

Sauté some green apple wedges in a little oil, and add a little brown sugar and rum. For more drama, light a match to the mixture. Use while hot.

RED PEPPER AND ZUCCHINI FRITTATA

Frittatas are nothing more than giant deep-dish omelets, cut into wedges. Although the principle is always the same—pour a mixture of milk and eggs over sautéed vegetables, start it on a stovetop and finish it in the oven—the variations are endless. Use any filling that appeals to you, combining 2–3 items: sautéed leeks, mushrooms, spinach, kale, etc.; grated VeganRella cheese; boiled cubed potatoes; cubed smoked turkey or cooked chicken; or minced fresh herbs such as chives, dill, parsley, chervil. Frittatas are delicious hot or cold and make a great main course, as well as great hors d'oeuvres, cut in small squares.

Makes 6 main course servings

1/4 cup olive oil
1 large onion, diced small
4 cloves garlic, minced
1 large red bell pepper, diced small
3 thin zucchini, diced small
3 tablespoons flour, any flour
1 cup soy or other non-dairy milk (rice, almond, grain, oat)
1/4 cup dry vermouth (liquor stores) or sake (health food stores)
1/4 cup basil leaves, packed, chopped
Good pinch nutmeg
Salt and pepper to taste
8 eggs, lightly beaten

Preheat the oven to 375 °F.

Heat the oil in an oven-proof skillet, about 10 inches in diameter. Add the onion, garlic, pepper, and zucchini, and sauté until all liquids evaporate. In a mixing bowl, whisk together the flour and the milk until smooth. Add the remaining ingredients and whisk. Pour uniformly over the sautéed mixture in the skillet and cook on a medium-low flame about 5 minutes. Transfer to the oven and bake another 12 to 15 minutes, until puffy and barely set. Serve warm or at room temperature.

SALMON TOMATO QUICHE

Although this quiche is delicious as it is, you might want to make it more decadent by grating 1 cup of VeganRella cheese into the batter.

Makes 6 main course servings

Crust

2 cups flour of your choice: all-purpose, pastry, spelt, oat, etc.
1/2 teaspoon salt
1/2 cup non-hydrogenated margarine (health-food stores)
4 tablespoons ice water, or slightly more if needed

Filling

3 tablespoons olive oil
1 large onion
4 large cloves garlic
1 large tomato, seeded and diced small
1/2 cup dry white wine
1/4 cup soy or rice milk powder
3/4 cup soy or other non-dairy milk (rice, grain, oat, almond)
2 eggs, or 4 egg whites if you are watching your cholesterol intake
1/4 cup shredded basil leaves, packed
Salt and pepper to taste (you might need very little or no salt)
1 15-ounce can red salmon (make sure it is *red salmon*), thoroughly drained and flaked, or 2 cups fresh cooked flaked salmon
1/2 cup sliced oil-cured black olives

VEGETARIAN QUICHE

For a totally vegetarian quiche, omit the tomato, salmon, and olives, and add 3 cups sautéed vegetables, in any combination: mushrooms, spinach, leeks, zucchini, etc., and stir in 1 cup grated VeganRella cheese, if desired.

Preheat the oven to 375 °F.

Make the crust: Pulse the flour, salt, and margarine in a food processor until the mixture resembles coarse meal. Add the water and pulse again, 2–3 times, no more. Wrap the dough in plastic and refrigerate one hour. If you don't have that hour available, roll it out right then, but handle minimally so the dough doesn't warm up on contact; remember, the secret of a good crust is to chill it. Roll out the dough to a 15-inch circle and place without stretching in a 10-inch pie plate. Press on the edges of the plate to cut out any excess dough. Crimp the edges with your fingers. Prick the bottom all over with a fork. Bake for about 20 minutes.

Meanwhile make the filling: Heat the oil in a skillet. In a food processor, coarsely grind the onion and garlic. Add the ground mixture to the hot oil and sauté until translucent. Add the diced tomato and sauté 1 more minute. Transfer the mixture to a mixing bowl. Add all the remaining ingredients and whisk thoroughly (if using cheese, add it at this point). Pour the mixture into the partially baked shell and bake 30 more minutes, or until puffy and barely firm. Serve hot.

REINVENTING CREAM

For a richer texture, I use a simple trick to augment the "milk" fats in many dishes: I add soy or rice milk powder to my non-dairy milks to obtain the rich and dense texture of cream, or quite close. It is also much less caloric than the dishes containing dairy cream.

SALMON MOUSSE

This dish was born on the day I ruined the fish course for a large dinner by using a tiny and cute but treacherously hot pepper—Habanero: I still shudder at the mere mention of the name! Rather than sit and cry at the thought of the beautiful dish I had to discard, I scanned my pantry and my refrigerator. This recipe is a real showcase for the wizardry of the food processor and is one of the rare cases when I use canned foods—not to save money, but to get something natural and fantastic in a pinch. I love canned salmon; just be certain that it is red salmon. And make sure the tuna is solid white. Don't say a word about the anchovies, and don't cringe at the idea of using the skin and bones; they will disappear, leaving only the lovely, smooth gelatinous texture we want for all molded dishes. Your ingredients must be bone-dry, or you will end up with a runny mess.

Makes 8 entrée servings, 12 appetizer servings, or 24 hors d'oeuvres

1 1/2 cups instant potato flakes, preferably organic (health food stores)
3/4 cup boiling water
1 15-ounce can red salmon, drained and squeezed thoroughly dry
1 6-ounce can solid white tuna, packed in oil, undrained
1 2-ounce can anchovies, drained, rinsed, and squeezed thoroughly dry
8 ounces Tofutti brand cream cheese
2 good-quality bottled roasted red peppers, patted dry
6–8 sprigs dill, fronds and stems
1/2 small red onion
2 tablespoons green peppercorns, drained and patted dry
1 tablespoon grated lemon zest
1 tablespoon lemon juice
1 tablespoon paprika
Good pinch cayenne
Good pinch nutmeg

Assorted crackers

Capers or gherkins, for garnish

In a small bowl, quickly mix the potato flakes and the boiling water with a fork until no flakes are apparent and the mixture looks like play dough. Let the potato mixture steep for a few minutes while you prepare the other ingredients. Place the salmon, tuna, anchovies, cream cheese, roasted peppers, dill, onion, green peppercorns, lemon zest, lemon juice, paprika, cayenne, and nutmeg in a food processor. Add the potato mixture and process for one full minute, until the mixture is completely smooth.

Pour into a greased mold lined with plastic wrap, or pour directly into the bowl you intend to serve the mousse in, and chill for a few hours until firm. Pull up the plastic wrap for easy unmolding and slice.

Serve as a spread for hors d'oeuvres on bread or crackers and garnish with capers or gherkins.

EGGS BENEDICT

This dish is typically verboten both for our dairy-intolerant friends and for everyone who keeps kosher and can't combine dairy and meat products in one meal, let alone in one dish. I am always told how wonderful it is. Being quite dogged and a nutrition purist, I decided to experiment to find my own non-dairy, kosher-friendly, and, best of all, lean and quick version. I turned this off-limits dish into a treat you can guiltlessly enjoy. Use the Hollandaise sauce on asparagus or poached chicken breasts, or as a dip with a little added curry powder—no one will ever know they are eating something that is so good for them. Never mind what the heavy-cream-egg-yolks Hollandaise sauce aficionados will say: this works, and that's what counts. A friend of mine who had just undergone heart surgery told me how delighted he was to be reunited with this great favorite food of his. Talk about getting to one's heart through one's stomach!

Makes 4 servings

Hollandaise Sauce

Makes 1 1/2 cups

1 cup unflavored soy yogurt
1/4 cup Dijon-style mustard
1/4 cup low fat mayonnaise
1 teaspoon turmeric
Pinch nutmeg
Pinch cayenne
Salt and pepper to taste

2 tablespoons olive oil
8 eggs
8 slices good whole grain bread
16 thin slices smoked turkey (or smoked salmon if you prefer)
1/4 cup thinly sliced chives

Whisk first seven ingredients until smooth and set aside.

Heat the oil in a large skillet. Add the eggs gently and at a little distance from one another. Cook them 2–3 minutes on a medium flame, until barely set.

To assemble: Place 2 slices bread on each of 4 plates. Top each slice of bread with 2 slices smoked turkey or salmon. Top with 1 egg. Top with the sauce. Sprinkle with the chives. Serve while the eggs are hot.

SOY YOGURT

While it is not, in my opinion, good enough to eat plain, it lends itself to many wonderful combinations and takes on the other great flavors it is paired with.

MARINATED TOMATO AND TOFU SALAD

This salad is amazingly like its dairy counterpart using mozzarella or goat cheese, thanks to the capacity of the tofu to absorb the marinade flavors so thoroughly.

Makes 12 servings

1 pound extra-firm tofu, cut in 1-inch cubes
3 firm, ripe tomatoes, or 6 plum tomatoes, seeded and cut in wedges
1 cup sun-dried tomatoes, briefly soaked in cold water, squeezed thoroughly dry, and cut into slivers
1/4 medium red onion, very thinly sliced
4 large cloves garlic, minced
1/2 cup fresh basil leaves, cut in thin strips
2 tablespoons tiny capers
1/2 cup niçoise olives
3/4 cup olive oil
1/3 cup red wine vinegar
1 tablespoon coarsely ground black pepper
Salt: you might need very little, if any; remember, the sun-dried tomatoes, capers, and olives are salty
2 bunches arugula, washed, spun-dried, and torn into bite size pieces

Place the tofu, tomato wedges, sun-dried tomatoes, onion, garlic, basil, capers, olives, olive oil, vinegar, black pepper, and salt in a mixing bowl and combine gently. Marinate 2 to 5 hours. Just before serving, add the arugula, toss gently, and serve at room temperature.

GARLIC

Just around the time I thought I had exhorted the crowds ad nauseam about the all-importance of using fresh garlic and that I would give the matter a little rest, one of my demo guests asked, "If I ever run out of garlic powder, can I settle for fresh garlic? Would that be okay?" What do **you** think?

FRUITED NOODLE PUDDING

Simple and delicious! I was looking for ways to give this humble old-world Jewish favorite (Lukshen Kugel) more status and notoriety, so with a little yuppie magic I upgraded it from a breakfast comfort food to a more prestigious dinner side dish, and I watch it disappear each time with pleasure. If you are avoiding wheat, do not hesitate to use rice noodles.

Makes a dozen servings

12 ounces thin noodles, boiled until barely tender and thoroughly drained
1 cup Tofutti brand sour cream
1 cup soy yogurt
1 cup soy or other non-dairy milk (rice, oat, almond, grain)
1/4 cup vegetable oil
4 eggs
Salt and pepper to taste

1 cup crushed canned pineapple, juice and all
1/2 cup golden raisins
1/2 cup brown sugar or other natural sugar (sucanat, rapadura, etc.)
1 teaspoon cinnamon

Preheat the oven to 350 ºF.

Mix the first set of ingredients together in a bowl. Make a well in the center and add the pineapple, raisins, sugar, and cinnamon. Combine thoroughly. Pour the batter into a greased 9×13-inch baking pan and bake for about 1 hour. Serve hot.

Variations

Spinach noodle kugel

Use only the first set of ingredients. Add a 10-ounce box frozen spinach squeezed thoroughly dry and a grated medium onion.

Carrot noodle kugel

Omit the pineapple. Add 2 cups of grated carrots, packed, and 1 grated medium onion.

RICE NOODLES

I love 'em! They get ready on the spot and are much better for you than their wheat counterparts because they contain no gluten and much less starch. There is no noodle dish I don't substitute rice noodles for: Pad Thai, spaghetti and meatballs, cold sesame noodles, to name a few. Just boil water in a large pot, turn off the heat and drop the rice noodles in, let the mixture sit for about 5 minutes, then drain the noodles and cut them in smaller pieces with scissors, and proceed with the recipe.

Soups

- 🍽 **Corn and salmon chowder**
- 🍽 **Vichyssoise**
- 🍽 **Wild mushroom soup**
- 🍽 **Cream of watercress and asparagus soup**
- 🍽 **Cold yogurt fruit soup**
- 🍽 **Chilled avocado cucumber soup**
- 🍽 **Curried white vegetable soup**
- 🍽 **Minted escarole pea soup**
- 🍽 **Roasted tomato soup**
- 🍽 **French onion soup**
- 🍽 **Curried squash sweet potato soup**

CORN AND SALMON CHOWDER

Funky meets elegant. With a good baguette and a leafy salad, this chowder makes a different and delicious meal in itself. Try your best to use fresh corn. Scraping off the kernels couldn't be easier. Stand each ear on a plate and use a sharp knife to scrape off the kernels, cutting as close to the cob as you can.

Makes about 12 servings

1/4 cup olive oil
3 leeks, white parts only, washed thoroughly and sliced
1 medium onion, quartered
4 ribs celery, peeled
6 large cloves garlic
1 small bunch flat parsley, stems and all, minced
2 quarts (8 cups) water
2 cups dry white wine
2 2-ounce cans flat anchovies, undrained
4 cups corn kernels, preferably fresh, from about 6 ears of corn (use frozen if necessary)
2 good pinches saffron
6 bay leaves
Salt (you might not need any. If you do, add more rinsed anchovies) and freshly ground black pepper to taste
2 cups soy or other non-dairy milk (rice, grain, oat, almond)
Good pinch nutmeg
Good pinch cayenne
3 pounds salmon filet cut in 1-inch cubes
1 pound mock crab flakes (optional, but delicious. A natural fish product), chopped
2 cups Tofutti brand soy sour cream

Heat the oil in a large heavy pot. In a food processor, in batches if necessary, coarsely grind the leeks, onions, celery, garlic, and parsley. Add the ground mixture to the hot oil and sauté until translucent. Add the water, wine, anchovies, corn, saffron, bay leaves, salt, and pepper, and bring to a boil. Reduce to medium and cook, covered, for about 30 minutes. Add the soy milk, nutmeg, and cayenne, and cook until just hot, but do not boil or the mixture might curdle. Using an immersion blender dipped directly into the pot, purée about one third of the soup, leaving the rest chunky. Add the salmon cubes and the mock crab, if using, and sour cream, and cook for 1 to 2 more minutes, stirring gently to incorporate all additions. Serve hot.

ANCHOVIES

Don't tell your guests that this dish, or any dish for that matter, contains anchovies until after they polish it off. The anchovies disperse in the soup and leave no trace of their controversial heritage except for a deep, smoky flavor. I'm reminded of a wonderful headline from *The Philadelphia Inquirer:* "Anchovies: A blessing if disguised."

SAFFRON

Saffron threads are the stamen of the crocus flower and can be harvested only by hand, hence their reputation for being so costly. The good news is, you can ignore all those tiny, exorbitantly priced vials, and get yourself an ounce box at any specialty food store, which will be about twenty times cheaper and will stay good for a year.

VICHYSSOISE

Here's a great twist on an enduring French classic—and so simple to prepare. If you need to watch your starch intake, substitute a large celery knob for the potatoes (as I often do just for variety), and you will be amazed at the results. Although vichyssoise is traditionally served chilled, I find it just as interesting hot.

Makes about 12 servings

1/3 cup extra-virgin olive oil
1 large onion, quartered
3 large leeks, white parts only, sliced, washed, and dried
4 ribs celery, peeled
4 large white-skin potatoes, peeled and cut in large chunks
4 cups water
1 cup dry white wine
1 cup white miso paste (health food stores)
1 sprig fresh tarragon, leaves only, or 1 tablespoon dry
3 cups soy or other non-dairy milk (rice, grain, oat, almond)
Good pinch nutmeg
1/4 cup chopped chives
Freshly ground pepper to taste

Heat the oil in a heavy pot. In a food processor, coarsely grind the onion, leeks, and celery. Add the ground mixture to the hot oil, and sauté until translucent. Add the potatoes, water, wine, miso, and tarragon, and bring to a boil. Reduce the heat to medium, cover, and cook for about 30 minutes. Add the milk and nutmeg and heat again, but do not let the soup boil or the milk will curdle. Blend the mixture in a blender or with an immersion blender until it is completely smooth. Add the chives and pepper. Adjust the texture and seasonings. Serve hot or chilled.

BROTH OR STOCK

I have a deliciously and nutritiously simple way to get around the pesky step of preparing a chicken broth or stock as a base for this soup and several others. Add white wine and white miso paste and instantly get rewarded with a whole new layer of flavor. For beef flavor, use red wine and dark miso paste.

IMMERSION BLENDER

A wonderfully nifty tool, inexpensive and portable (it will fit in a drawer) that allows you to blend your soup directly and in one shot in your pot. No transferring, no mess. Just make sure there are no bones in the soup, or you will break your blade.

WILD MUSHROOM SOUP

Although I include here only mushrooms that are easily available and affordable, and although the soup is fabulous as is, the day you want to go all out, substitute more luxurious mushrooms in place of the ones listed. Even in small amounts, just an ounce or two, they make a dramatic difference and produce a memorable treat: chanterelles, morels, porcini, etc.

Makes a dozen servings

1 1/2 pounds shitaki mushrooms, stems discarded, caps sliced
1 cup dry sherry or mirin
1/3 cup olive oil
1 1/2 pounds domestic mushrooms, caps sliced, stems chopped
2 medium-size onions, chopped
1/2 dozen shallots, minced
1/3 cup flour (any flour)
2/3 cup dark miso paste
2 quarts (8 cups) boiling water
3 sprigs fresh thyme, leaves only
Good pinch saffron threads
1 sprig tarragon, leaves only, chopped
4 bay leaves
3 cups soy milk
Ground pepper to taste

Soak the shitaki in the sherry about half an hour. Remove the shitaki with a slotted spoon and reserve the sherry.

Heat the olive oil in a heavy pot and in it sauté the sliced mushroom caps (shitaki and domestic) until all liquids evaporate. Remove the sautéed mushrooms with a slotted spoon and reserve. In the same pot, adding a few drops of oil if necessary, sauté the chopped mushroom stems, onions, and shallots until all liquids evaporate. Add the flour and cook on a low flame two to three minutes until the flour turns light brown. Raise the heat again, add miso, and whisk. Add the water gradually, whisking. Add the reserved sherry, thyme, saffron, tarragon, bay leaves, and salt and pepper to taste. Cook covered on medium flame for about 30 minutes. Purée with an immersion blender until smooth. Return to the pot, add the reserved mushroom slices, the soy milk and pepper, and heat through. Adjust the consistency and seasonings. Do not let the soup boil or it will curdle. Serve hot. Delicious cold too.

COOKING WINE

I beg you, please don't! No cooking wine or cooking sherry. That would be just dreadful. Selling you real quality liquor and wines is the raison d'être of all liquor stores, and they will charge you the same price you are paying for a hideous imitation that precipitates any dish to its ruin. No need to get anything expensive, just real. Mirin, a wonderful rice wine, is readily available and does a great job as well.

CREAM OF WATERCRESS AND ASPARAGUS SOUP

Asparagus and watercress vie for first place in this luxurious yet simple soup. I love to make it for Passover, when asparagus is plentiful; in this case replace the tapioca with potato starch in equal amounts.

Makes a dozen servings

1/3 cup olive oil
3 large leeks, white parts and tender green parts, sliced
2 medium onions, quartered
6 medium shallots
10 cups water
1 cup dry white wine
1 large head celery root, grated
2 pounds asparagus, tough ends discarded, cut into 2-inch sections
Salt to taste
8 cups watercress, packed, stems and all (about 3 bunches)
1/4 cup fresh chives
1/2 teaspoon nutmeg
1/4 cup tapioca flour (Passover: substitute potato starch), mixed with a little cold water until smooth
Pepper to taste

Heat the olive oil in a heavy pot. In a food processor, coarsely grind the leeks, onions, and shallots. Add the ground mixture to the hot oil and sauté until the mixture is translucent. Add the water, wine, celery root, asparagus, and salt. Bring to a boil, reduce the flame to medium, and cook, covered, 30 minutes. Add the watercress, chives, nutmeg, tapioca mixture, and pepper, and cook just until the watercress wilts, about 2 to 3 minutes. Do not allow watercress to cook longer or it will get discolored. Cream the soup in batches in a blender or with an immersion blender until smooth. If after blending you still have some asparagus strings left in the soup, strain it through a medium strainer; this will only take a minute. Adjust the consistency and seasonings before serving. Serve hot. Delicious iced too.

TAPIOCA

I predict a great future—or comeback, to be exact—for tapioca in the U.S., just as other parts of the world have been enjoying its great versatility, emulsifying and gelling powers for centuries. Tapioca is the ground product of the Brazilian cassava root, essential to cooking and baking in South American countries. It is available in every way, shape, or form: flour, quick cooking pearls, small pearls, large pearls, you name it. I use it quite often because it gives me the creamy texture I want without getting cloudy or gummy, and has no objectionable taste whatsoever. It is easily found in health food stores.

COLD YOGURT FRUIT SOUP

You will do equally well serving this delightful soup as a first course, garnished with some mint leaves, or as a dessert, topped with a scoop of coconut sorbet. I think you can tell: I love soup in every way, shape, or form, anytime, anywhere!

Makes a dozen servings

4 cups soy milk
1/2 cup fresh lime or lemon juice
4 ripe kiwis
2 cups green grapes
2 wedges honeydew
2 Granny Smith apples, unpeeled
1 pound silken tofu
1/2 cup maple syrup
1 tablespoon grated lime zest
1/4 cup mint leaves, packed

Mix the soy milk with the lime in a bowl. The mixture will curdle. Set aside while you prepare the rest of the soup.

Dice half of the fruit small and set aside. In a blender or fruit processor, in batches if necessary, puree the remaining half of the fruit, the reserved soy milk mixture, the tofu, maple syrup, zest, and mint. Transfer the creamed mixture to a bowl. Fold in the reserved diced fruit. Chill completely. Garnish with slices of lime and mint sprigs.

CHILLED AVOCADO CUCUMBER SOUP

This is the one soup I don't like to make ahead of time, because the avocado turns an unappealing brownish color. When I do have to make it in advance, I prepare everything a day or two earlier except the avocado, which I blend and add to the mixture on the day it is served. Cucumbers, avocados, and jalapenos: one of the coolest and hottest food combos. Much cooler and hotter than the modest sum of its parts!

Makes a dozen servings

4 cups soy milk
1/4 cup fresh lemon or lime juice
4 medium ripe avocadoes, peeled and halved
4 ribs celery, peeled
2 jalapenos, seeded if you don't like it too hot
1 large seedless cucumber, peeled
1 large bunch dill, fronds and stems
1 medium red onion, quartered
Salt and pepper to taste

Mix the soy milk with the lemon juice in a bowl and set aside for just a minute or two. The mixture will curdle.

In a blender or food processor, mix all ingredients, including the soy mixture, in batches if necessary, until smooth. Thin the soup with iced water or soy milk if necessary. Chill and serve with a sprinkle of minced jalapeno and a slice of lemon of lime.

CURRIED WHITE VEGETABLE SOUP

I whipped up this soup on a day I was trying to make some room in my refrigerator for a large dinner I had to serve that night. Since I am always reluctant to try anything new and uncharted on company, I had planned on just sticking the finished soup in the freezer and carrying on with my dinner preparations, but it came out so well that I decided to give it a more honorable place and actually serve it to my guests that night. This soup is all white and creamy without the potatoes, and packed with flavor. Here the coconut milk provides the creaminess. Yum! And the best part is, no sautéing, no complicated steps.

Makes a dozen servings

1 head cauliflower, cut in florets, stems trimmed
2 medium turnips, cut in chunks
1 large head celery root, cut in chunks
2 onions, quartered
6 ribs celery, peeled
1 large bunch flat parsley
1/2 bunch cilantro, end stems cut off
2 sticks lemongrass, roughly chopped
1 pound frozen edemame or lima beans
1 tablespoon curry, more if you like it hotter
Salt to taste
1/4 cup olive oil
1 15-ounce can coconut milk

Bring 12 cups of water to boil in a heavy pot. Add all but last ingredient and bring to boil again. Reduce the flame to medium and cook, covered, 30 minutes. Add the coconut milk and cook for 30 more minutes. Cream the soup in a blender, or with an immersion blender. Adjust the texture and seasonings. Serve hot or chilled.

LOW CARBS

I would hate to add myself to the glut of people who feed you a barrage of information on low-carb foods, which leaves me, for one, confused and not an ounce thinner. Most manufacturing powers that be, only too happy that hardly anyone reads labels thoroughly, pounce on the diet darling du jour, totally disregard the whole nutrition picture, take each ingredient out of its context, and replace carbs in their products with sugar, emollients, and whatnot, most often making them more caloric and infinitely less tasty. Just try some low-carb peanut butter and you will immediately see what I mean: it tastes awful and has 30 more calories per serving. I ask you: who needs it? So, until the low-carb craze finally falls flat on its face (can't wait!), I thought you would be happy to know that all my soups, and most of my dishes, are naturally lower in carbs, and have always been, long before the craze began, without sacrificing any flavor, and certainly without substituting any other food "nemeses" for the carbs (sugar, fat, etc.). I simply, and liberally, avail myself of the whole wonderful gamut of natural produce, grains, thickeners, and sweeteners at my disposal!

MINTED ESCAROLE PEA SOUP

French cooking uses escarole lettuce quite often, not just in salads but cooked, which highlights its pleasant bitterness and pairs beautifully with milder ingredients such as peas and zucchini. Peas and mint have a natural affinity. This soup is luscious even if it sounds unpretentious, so do not hesitate to serve it to distinguished company, as I do!

Makes a dozen servings

1/3 cup olive oil
4 leeks, white parts and 2" of the green parts, sliced
4 ribs celery, peeled
1 small bunch flat parsley
1 large onion, quartered
1 large green zucchini, unpeeled, cut in large chunks
2 quarts (8 cups) water
4 cups frozen peas (try your best to find the peas labeled "petite"; they are the sweetest)
1 large head escarole, chopped
1/2 cup mint leaves, packed
Salt and pepper to taste
2 cups Tofutti brand sour cream

Heat the oil in a heavy pot. In a food processor, coarsely grind the leeks, celery, parsley, onion, and zucchini, and add the mixture to the hot oil. Sauté until translucent. Add all remaining ingredients except the sour cream and bring to a boil. Reduce the temperature to medium, and cook covered about 20 minutes. Add the cream and heat through. Cream the soup in a blender or with an immersion blender. Adjust the consistency and seasonings, and serve hot or chilled.

FROZEN FRUIT AND VEGETABLES

I have no quarrel with frozen peas, or any frozen (unprocessed of course) vegetables and fruit; au contraire! My mother, who dutifully and painstakingly shelled peas for dinner dishes quite often when we were growing up in Morocco, always comments on how lucky we are to find them, and quite a few other vegetables and fruit, cleaned, cut, ready to go, and every bit as delicious as fresh. Provided it is not otherwise "prepared," freezing captures all the freshness, sweetness, and flavor of many vegetables and fruit, without any loss of nutrients.

ROASTED TOMATO SOUP

Do not attempt to make this soup with canned tomatoes. Roasting them along with the other vegetables is all you have to do in order to make this soup delicious. Make it when good ripe tomatoes and basil are plentiful. The flavor of garlic mellows as it roasts.

Makes a dozen servings

Roasted Vegetables:

5 pounds tomatoes (7–8 large, or 16 plum), halved
3 heads garlic, points sliced off, leaving the cloves exposed
4 medium red onions, halved
3 red peppers, halved and seeded
1/4 cup olive oil
Coarse sea salt to taste

6 cups water
1/4 cup olive oil
1 cup dry white wine
2 cups tomato juice
1/4 cup tomato paste
1 tablespoon paprika
1 cup basil leaves, packed

2 good pinches saffron threads
Freshly ground pepper to taste
4 cups soy or other non-dairy milk (rice, almond, grain, oat)

Preheat the oven to 450 °F.

Mix the first set of ingredients in a bowl, spread on a cookie sheet, and roast for about 45 minutes, until the vegetables looked charred. When the garlic is cool enough to handle but still warm, squeeze the heads until all the pulp is forced out of its skin. Place all the roasted vegetables, including the garlic pulp, and all the remaining ingredients except the milk, in a wide heavy pot. Bring to a boil. Reduce the flame to medium and cook, covered, 30 minutes. Add the milk and cook until just heated through. Cream in a blender or with an immersion blender until perfectly smooth. Adjust seasonings and consistency. Serve hot or chilled.

FRENCH ONION SOUP

This is another challenge I was able to overcome, with flying colors. I know it sounds smug, but wait till you taste it! Besides, I have all the members of the onion family I need, and I am using them to the hilt, so no wonder it is so good even without the original dairy ingredients. If you are serving the soup in small individual crocks, do not stir the cheeses into the soup: ladle the hot soup into the crocks, float a slice of baguette on top, sprinkle the cheese over all, and run the crocks under the broiler for just a minute or two. Use the food processor to slice the onions and shallots and mince the garlic in a jiffy.

Makes a dozen servings

1/3 cup extra virgin olive oil
2 large onions, sliced very thin
4 large shallots, sliced very thin
2 large leeks, white parts only, sliced very thin
6 large cloves garlic, minced
3 tablespoons sugar
2 cups dry red wine (liquor stores)
1/2 cup dark miso paste (health food stores)
6 sprigs thyme, leaves only
2 1/2 quarts (10 cups) water
Good pinch nutmeg
2 cups grated VeganRella cheddar cheese
1 cup grated VeganRella mozzarella cheese
Salt and freshly grated ground pepper (use the salt sparingly if at all; the cheeses and the miso are already salty)

A dozen slices baguette, cut on bias, toasted. (375 °F oven, for about 20 minutes, until light brown)

Heat the oil in a heavy pot, and in it fry the onions, shallots, leeks, and garlic on a medium flame, about 30 minutes, until dark. Add the sugar and cook two more minutes until caramelized. Add the wine, miso, thyme, and water and cook another 30 minutes. Add the cheeses, nutmeg, salt and pepper, and cook another minute, until the cheeses are all melted. Adjust the consistency and seasonings.

To serve: pour into soup bowls and float one slice toasted baguette in each bowl.

CURRIED SQUASH SWEET POTATO SOUP

Sweet and spicy at its best! Do not be daunted by the long cooking time of the onions; they need very little maintenance, and their caramelizing is the main secret of the intriguing flavor of this delicious soup.

Makes a dozen servings

1/3 cup olive oil
2 large onions, chopped, about 3 cups
1/4 cup brown sugar, packed (substitute any other, natural sugar, like sucanat or rapadura: health food stores)
3 quarts (12 cups) water
1 butternut squash, or kombucha squash, about 3 pounds, peeled, seeded, and cut in large chunks
2 medium sweet potatoes, peeled and cut in large chunks
2 large carrots, peeled and cut in large chunks
1 tablespoon curry, or a little more if you like it hot
1 teaspoon allspice
1 stalk lemongrass, chopped
1-inch piece ginger, peeled and minced
1 tablespoon cinnamon
1 15-ounce can coconut milk

Heat the oil in a heavy pot. Add the onions and fry on a medium flame, stirring occasionally, until dark, about thirty minutes. Add the sugar and cook, stirring, 2 more minutes. Add all the remaining ingredients except the coconut milk, and bring to a boil. Reduce the flame to medium and cook, covered, one hour. Add the coconut milk and heat through. Cream in a blender or with an immersion blender. Adjust the consistency and seasonings. Serve hot.

LEMONGRASS

These long thin stalks have a magic fragrance, reminiscent of lemon, ginger, and verbena all at once. If it is hard to find in your neighborhood, get a couple bunches when you do find it, remove the tough outer leaves from the stalks, cut the stalks in chunks and grind them in a food processor. Put the ground mixture in a ziplock bag and freeze. Take out the bag and scrape off the amount needed in your recipe, sealing the bag each time before replacing in the freezer.

Main Courses

- 🍽 Baked cauliflower au gratin
- 🍽 Linguini with wild mushroom sauce
- 🍽 Pizza puttanesca
- 🍽 Spinach lasagna
- 🍽 Bread artichoke fennel casserole
- 🍽 Black bean burritos with guacamole
- 🍽 Tilapia stuffed with spinach and pine nuts
- 🍽 Curried fish and tomatoes
- 🍽 Chicken Tandoori
- 🍽 Chicken breasts in mustard cream sauce
- 🍽 Beef stroganoff
- 🍽 Lamb moussaka

BAKED CAULIFLOWER AU GRATIN

This is a great French favorite and a wonderful way to dress up the unpretentious cauliflower and end up with a rustic yet elegant dish. For a more colorful presentation, use a combination of cauliflower and broccoli. For faster results, use 2 1/2 pounds frozen chopped cauliflower or a cauliflower-broccoli combination. This dish reheats very nicely, making it perfect for buffets.

Makes 8 servings

2 heads cauliflower, cut in small florets, stems trimmed and sliced
3 tablespoons olive oil
1 medium onion, quartered
3 shallots, quartered
3 tablespoons flour, any flour you like
1 cup dry white wine
1 cup soy or other non-dairy milk (rice, grain, oat, almond)
Good pinch nutmeg
Salt and pepper to taste
1 cup grated VeganRella cheddar cheese

Bring water to boil in a large pot. Add the cauliflower and cook until tender but still firm, about 5 minutes. Drain thoroughly, dry with paper towels, and set aside.

Preheat the broiler.

Heat the oil in a heavy skillet. In a food processor, coarsely grind the onion and shallots, and sauté until translucent. Lower the heat and add the flour. Cook, whisking, 2–3 minutes, until light brown. Raise the heat again and add the wine and milk in a slow stream, whisking constantly to avoid lumps, until the mixture thickens, 2 to 3 minutes. Add the nutmeg, salt, and pepper and stir until combined. Pour the vegetables in a greased 9×13 pan. Pour the sauce over them. Sprinkle the cheese over all. Place the pan under the broiler, about 6 inches away from the flame, about 10 minutes, until nicely colored and bubbly. Serve hot.

LINGUINI WITH WILD MUSHROOM SAUCE

Are you, like me, a mushroom lover? Here is your chance to go all out and add a few expensive wild mushrooms to the listed shitaki and portobello, when you come across them at the market (and when you can afford them!). The good news is, a little goes a long way. An ounce of chopped chanterelles, morels, or porcini will make this dish even more wonderful. You can use this sauce on other dishes than pasta, like poached chicken breasts or grilled fish. Try your best to use fresh thyme and tarragon—there is nothing like fresh herbs. For a less starchy dish, or just for variety, substitute buckwheat noodles or rice noodles for the pasta—the buckwheat noodles cook just like regular noodles, and the rice noodles don't cook at all: just dip them in a pot of boiling water (heat turned off) 5 minutes, drain, and cut smaller with scissors.

Makes 8 servings

1 pound linguini or fettuccini boiled and drained
1/2 cup cooking water reserved
1/2 cup extra-virgin olive oil
6 cloves garlic
1 medium onion, quartered
4 medium shallots, quartered
2 tablespoons sugar
1 pound shitaki mushrooms, caps only, sliced
1 pound portobello mushrooms, stems and caps, sliced
1 cup dry sherry (liquor stores)
Salt and freshly ground pepper to taste
1 sprig fresh tarragon, chopped, or 1 teaspoon dry
3 sprigs fresh thyme, leaves only, or 1 teaspoon dry
3 tablespoons tapioca flour1 cup soy or other non-dairy milk (rice, grain, oat, almond)

Heat the oil in a large, heavy skillet. In a food processor, finely grind the garlic. Add the onion and shallots and grind coarsely. Add the ground mixture to the hot oil, and sauté until translucent. Add the sugar and sauté one more minute, until the mixture caramelizes. Add all the mushrooms and sauté until most liquids evaporate. Add the sherry, salt and pepper, tarragon and thyme, and cook 5 more minutes. Whisk the tapioca flour with the milk in a little bowl until smooth, and add to the skillet. Cook 2–3 more minutes. Add the boiled pasta and heat the whole dish through. If necessary, thin with some of the reserved noodle cooking water (wheat and buckwheat noodles will absorb more liquid than rice noodles). Serve hot.

PIZZA PUTTANESCA

I used to have qualms about making non-dairy pizza at my demos, fearing my students might find my suggestion slightly disingenuous, until one of them recently exclaimed: "Why can't we find cheeseless pizza in the States, just as we do in Europe? Where is it written that pizza must always have cheese?" Traditionally, only a few pizza varieties are topped with cheese, or even tomatoes. There are quite a few wonderful toppings you can choose from: olives, anchovies, onions, artichoke hearts, eggs, roasted peppers, mushrooms, meatballs; you name it. I chose my favorite topping (which doubles as a great pasta sauce), but use your imagination, even adding a cup or more of grated VeganRella cheese if you like. Either way, nothing will beat the fun and flavor of homemade—nothing! In a pinch use some store-bought frozen and thawed pizza dough, and just make the sauce.

Makes a dozen servings

Dough

2 tablespoons dry yeast
2 cups warm water
1 tablespoon sugar
5 cups flour
1 teaspoon salt
1/4 cup olive oil

To make the dough: Mix the yeast, water, and sugar in a bowl. Let the mixture rest about 5 minutes, or until it starts bubbling. Add the remaining ingredients and mix. Turn out onto a lightly floured board and knead by hand or in a dough maker about 10 minutes. Cover the dough and let it rise about 1 hour in a draft-free place. Roll out the dough very thin (about 1 large greased cookie sheet or 1 greased 18-inch round pan), leaving a slightly thicker rim all around.

Preheat the oven to 475 °F. Spread the sauce (recipe follows) on the dough, leaving the rim blank. Bake about 15 minutes. If using the cheese, add it in the last 5 minutes of baking. Cut in wedges and serve hot.

Puttanesca Sauce

1/2 cup extra virgin olive oil
1 large onion, chopped
8 large cloves garlic, minced
1 cup dry white wine
1 cup sun-dried tomatoes, briefly soaked in warm water, and cut into strips
3 cups canned crushed tomatoes
1/4 cup capers
1/2 cup oil-cured black olives, halved
A dozen anchovies, thoroughly rinsed
1/2 cup basil leaves, minced
2 tablespoons oregano
Good pinch red pepper flakes
Salt and freshly cracked pepper to taste (taste the sauce before you add any salt)

Optional: About 1 cup grated VeganRella to taste

To make the sauce: Heat the oil in a heavy pan. Add the onions and fry until translucent. Add the garlic and fry 3 more minutes. Reduce the heat and add all remaining ingredients. Cook covered on a medium flame about 10 minutes.

FOCCACIA

Roll the dough about 1/2 inch thick and place in a greased cookie sheet. Brush lightly with olive oil, and sprinkle with sea salt, minced fresh onion or garlic (optional), and chopped fresh rosemary. Poke the dough all over with your finger to make indentations. Bake in a preheated 400 °F about 20 minutes.

SPINACH LASAGNA

Being wary of cheese, especially cooked. I wasn't able to enjoy this treat until I came up with this fabulous recipe. If you decide to add grated VeganRella cheese, sprinkle it in the last 20 minutes of baking, when you uncover it. Follow the boring but clear assembly instructions exactly!

Makes 10 servings

1/3 cup olive oil
1 large onion, quartered
6 large cloves garlic
4 10-ounce boxes frozen chopped spinach, thawed and squeezed thoroughly dry
2 tablespoons dry oregano
1/2 cup basil leaves, packed and chopped
Salt and freshly ground black pepper to taste
1 pound silken tofu, drained
8 ounces Tofutti brand cream cheese
1 cup soy or other non-dairy milk (rice, oat, grain, almond)
2 large eggs
5 cups tomato sauce
1 pound lasagna noodles, cooked according to package directions until barely tender and thoroughly drained (better yet, look for the ones that need no precooking)
Optional: 1 to 2 cups grated VeganRella cheese

Preheat oven to 375 °F.

Heat the oil in a large skillet. In a food processor, coarsely grind the onion and garlic. Add the ground mixture to the hot oil, and sauté over medium heat until translucent, about 2 minutes. Add the spinach, oregano, basil, salt, and pepper. Combine and set aside. Purée the tofu, cream cheese, soy milk, and eggs in a food processor until smooth. Set aside.

Assemble the lasagna: Pour a thin layer of the tomato sauce in the bottom of a 9×13-inch lasagna pan. Top with a layer of noodles slightly overlapping; top with half the spinach mixture; top with half the tofu mixture; top with one layer of noodles slightly overlapping; top with half the remaining tomato sauce; top with one layer of noodles; top with the remaining spinach mixture; top with the remaining tofu mixture; top with the remaining noodles; top with the remaining tomato sauce.

Bake, covered, for 30 minutes. Uncover (add the cheese at this point, if using) and bake for 20 minutes more. Do not overbake, or the dish will be dry. Let the lasagna rest for 15 minutes before cutting and serving.

CREAM CHEESE

Make sure you use only Tofutti brand cream cheese. All other non-dairy cream cheese brands look like spackle, and taste like it, too, but this one is perfect.

BREAD ARTICHOKE FENNEL CASSEROLE

I have grouped some of my favorite veggies for this delicate and delightful dish. Thanks to the food processor, which makes short work of chopping, mincing, slicing, and grating vegetables and herbs, it will be a snap to assemble.

Makes 8 servings

3 cups soy or other non-dairy milk (rice, grain, oat, almond)
6 eggs
1 cup Tofutti brand cream cheese
6 cups day-old bread cubes, packed
1 large head fennel, sliced very thin
1 large head celery root, grated
4 leeks, white parts only, sliced very thin
1 large onion, sliced very thin
1 10-ounce box frozen artichoke hearts, thawed and chopped coarsely
6 large cloves garlic, minced

1 bunch dill, fronds and stems, minced
Good pinch nutmeg
Salt and pepper to taste

Preheat the oven to 375 °F.

In a mixing bowl, whisk together the milk, eggs, and cream cheese. Add the bread cubes and combine thoroughly. Add all remaining ingredients and combine.

Pour the mixture into a greased 9×13-inch baking dish. Bake about 35 minutes, until the casserole looks golden and puffy. Serve hot.

BLACK BEAN BURRITOS WITH GUACAMOLE

I whip up my BBB recipe, as I call it, whenever company is coming on short notice. If you don't have the burritos or corn tortillas on hand, simply put the filling in a bowl, and let everyone dig in, with corn chips and guacamole. Chocolate, cheese, and beer: how can you miss? Still, if you would like to make this a meat dish, simply add a pound lean chopped beef and sauté it with the onion mixture. Either way, it's fun and delicious.

Makes 8 servings

Burritos

3 tablespoons olive oil
1 large onion, quartered
4 large cloves garlic
1 jalapeno pepper, minced (more if you like it hot)
2 ribs celery, peeled
1 bunch flat parsley
1/2 bunch cilantro, leaves only
2 cups canned crushed tomatoes
1 cup beer, dark or light
3 cups canned black beans, rinsed
2 tablespoons chili powder
1 tablespoon oregano
2 teaspoons cumin
Salt to taste (go easy, you might need only very little if at all; the canned beans and the cheese are salty)
1/3 cup semisweet real chocolate chips, best quality
2/3 cup VeganRella grated cheddar
A dozen, or a couple more, store-bought burritos or corn tortillas

Garnishes

1/2 cup Tofutti brand sour cream
1/2 cup chopped tomatoes
1/2 cup minced flat parsley

Heat the oil in a heavy pot. In a food processor, coarsely grind the onion, garlic, jalapeno, celery, parsley, and cilantro. Add to the hot oil and sauté until translucent. Add the tomatoes, beer, beans, chili powder, oregano, cumin, and salt. Bring to a boil. Reduce the heat to medium-low and cook, covered, 20 minutes. Stir in the chocolate chips and the cheese and cook 5 more minutes.

Fill the tortillas with the filling while it is hot and roll, placing them seam side down as you go. Top with all the garnishes. Serve with guacamole (recipe follows).

Guacamole

3 ripe avocados, mashed
3 tablespoons finely chopped red onion
Juice of 1 lime or lemon
2 tablespoons chopped cilantro
Bottled hot sauce to taste
Salt and pepper to taste

Mix all ingredients in a bowl. If you are making guacamole ahead of time, be sure to save it with the avocado pits in the bowl, which prevents their discoloration. Remove the pits just before serving time. Makes about 3 cups.

TILAPIA STUFFED WITH SPINACH AND PINE NUTS

This stuffing is so fabulous you might consider using it for chicken breasts or as a sauce for pasta, thinned with a little non-dairy milk or white wine. Do not skip the pine nuts, as they add a wonderful layer of flavor. For a more dramatic presentation, consider stuffing a whole large fish such as trout or bass, and proceed with the recipe (in this case, bake one hour). If you are serving this dish as a first course, simply halve each roll.

Makes 8 main course servings

Spinach Stuffing

1/4 cup olive oil
1 large onion, quartered
4 large shallots, peeled
6 large cloves garlic, peeled
1 red pepper, seeded and quartered
1 small bunch parsley
1 large tomato, peeled, seeded, and chopped
1 10-ounce box frozen spinach, thawed and squeezed thoroughly dry
1/4 cup basil leaves, packed, chopped
1/3 cup pine nuts, toasted 10 minutes in a 300 °F oven
1/2 cup VeganRella cheddar cheese
Good pinch nutmeg
Salt and pepper to taste

8 fillets of tilapia, about 6 ounces each

Vegetable spray
Paprika

Preheat the oven to 375 °F.

Heat the oil in a heavy skillet. In a food processor, coarsely grind the onion, shallots, garlic, and parsley, and add to the skillet. Sauté until most of the liquids evaporate. Add the tomato and fry one more minute, until all liquids evaporate. Transfer the mixture to a bowl. Add the remaining stuffing ingredients and mix thoroughly. Stuff each fillet with some of the mixture and roll tightly. Place the fillet seam side down in a baking dish just large enough to hold all the fillets in one layer, so the stuffing doesn't ooze out. Repeat with the remaining fillets and stuffing (you might have a little stuffing left over). Spray the rolls with vegetable spray and sprinkle with paprika. Bake about 30 minutes, or a little longer, until the fish flakes easily. Serve hot, or at room temperature.

CURRIED FISH AND TOMATOES

Another treat, which owes its creaminess to coconut milk. Use only thick fish fillets, as thin fillets such as sole or flounder can't withstand the longer cooking time without falling apart. Besides, there is no need to use such expensive cuts in this dish.

Makes 8 main course servings

1/4 cup olive oil
1 large onion, chopped
1 2-inch piece ginger, peeled and minced
1 tablespoon curry, or more to taste
1 teaspoon ground cumin
1 jalapeno pepper, minced (if you don't like it too hot, seed it first)
2 large tomatoes, chopped
1 stalk lemongrass, minced
2 large medium-ripe plantains peeled and cut into 1-inch cubes
Salt to taste
2 cups water
1 cup coconut milk
3 pounds thick fish fillet: (scrod, sea trout, tilapia, halibut, etc.), cut into two-inch cubes
3 tablespoons chopped cilantro

Heat the oil in a heavy, wide-bottom pan. Add the onion and ginger and sauté until translucent. Add curry, cumin, and jalapeno and sauté until fragrant, just one more minute. Add tomatoes, lemongrass, plantains, salt, and water and bring to a boil. Reduce the flame to medium and cook, covered, 20 minutes. Add the coconut milk, fish, and cilantro and cook, covered, 10 minutes or a little longer, until plantains and fish are tender. Serve hot, alone or over basmati or jasmine rice, with cucumber raita (p. 70)

CHICKEN TANDOORI

This lovely Indian grilled chicken dish is usually taboo to dairy-intolerant diners, because it contains yogurt, and to kosher diners, because it combines dairy and meat items. The very definition of Tandoori is marinated in yogurt or buttermilk. Making buttermilk by letting soy milk and lemon juice or vinegar curdle allows you to make and enjoy all those previously off-limits goodies! Please leave the skins on the chicken pieces; you can always remove them at eating time. They keep the chicken moist, tender, and presentable when done.

Makes 8 servings

1 cup soy milk
1 tablespoon lemon juice
3 tablespoons olive oil
2 tablespoons curry, a little more if you like it hotter
1/3 cup lemon juice or lime juice
Freshly ground black pepper to taste
1 medium onion, quartered
1 2-inch piece fresh ginger, peeled
5 chicken thighs, skin on
5 chicken drumsticks, skin on
3 chicken breasts, split, skin on
Pita bread

Combine the soy milk and the lemon juice in a large mixing bowl and reserve. In a food processor, place the olive oil, curry, lemon or lime juice, black pepper, onion, and ginger, and grind finely. You will obtain a slightly runny paste. Transfer this mixture to a mixing bowl with the reserved soy mixture. Make 1 or 2 gashes on the skin side of each of the chicken pieces, add them to the mixing bowl, and thoroughly mix all the ingredients in the bowl. Marinate overnight.

Discard the marinade and broil the chicken pieces for about 5 minutes on each side, or bake in a preheated 450 °F oven for about 30 minutes, until golden and tender (The breasts may be ready first, so be prepared to remove them a few minutes sooner). Serve hot with pita and Cucumber Raita.

Cucumber Raita

After you taste this wonderful condiment, you will understand the expression "cool as a cucumber." Creamy and crunchy, it offsets the fiery kick of your curries.

2 cups soy milk
1/4 cup lemon juice
Salt and freshly ground black pepper to taste
Red pepper flakes to taste, optional (omit if you want a mild raita)
3 scallions, sliced very thin (both white and green parts)
1/4 cup finely chopped mint leaves, packed
1–2 tablespoons sugar
2 large cucumbers, peeled, seeded, and coarsely grated

Combine the soy milk and lemon juice in a mixing bowl. The mixture will curdle. Add the salt, ground pepper, red pepper flakes, scallions, mint, sugar, and cucumber. Mix gently with a spoon, taking care not to extract any moisture from the cucumbers. Use with Chicken Tandoori and other curries. Makes about 3 1/2 cups.

SALT IN MEAT AND POULTRY DISHES

You will notice in all the following meat- and poultry-based recipes that salt is not listed as an ingredient. I have created them with kosher meat and poultry cuts, and since the process of making them kosher involves salting as one of the main steps, they are amply salted and do not require any additional salt.

CHICKEN BREASTS IN MUSTARD CREAM SAUCE

Another quick treat. The elegant look and taste of this dish belie its scant preparation time: it's ready in twenty minutes from start to finish. Make it even easier by using a skillet large enough to hold all the cutlets in one layer. Rolling the cutlets in flour and searing them first is the key to a thick, smooth sauce.

Makes 8 servings

1/3 cup olive oil
8 skinless chicken cutlets, pounded medium-thin, blotted thoroughly dry with paper towels
Flour, any kind
4 bay leaves, or 1/2 teaspoon ground
1 teaspoon turmeric
Ground pepper to taste
1 cup water
Juice and grated zest of 1 lemon
1/3 cup Tofutti brand sour cream
3 tablespoons Dijon style mustard
3 tablespoons thinly sliced chives

Heat the oil in a large, heavy skillet. Dredge the cutlets in flour, shaking off the excess. Add to the hot oil and sauté about 2 minutes on each side, until golden.

Add the bay leaves, turmeric, pepper, and water and bring to a boil. Reduce the heat to medium and cook, covered, 10 minutes. Whisk the lemon juice and zest, sour cream, and mustard in a bowl until smooth, stir in gently, and cook on a low flame just one more minute. Pour onto a platter and sprinkle the chives over all. Serve hot.

GROUND BAY LEAVES

If you happen to have a tiny food processor (very inexpensive) or spice grinder, grind a batch of bay leaves to a powder and store in a glass spice jar. It disperses very nicely in the dish, and you don't need to fish out the leaves.

BEEF STROGANOFF

I love to use London broil for this dish, as it is lean and tender and lends itself perfectly to the brief cooking time. The finished dish tastes every bit as rich and creamy as the original. (Yes, I have food spies. And yes, they work for food.) The addition of the mushrooms makes it unnecessary to come up with another side dish. It is ready in no time and smells as heavenly as it tastes. Keeping the meat well chilled makes the slicing much easier. Just remember, I can't beg you enough, no supermarket-variety cooking wine or sherry, please!

Makes 6–8 servings

4 tablespoons olive oil, divided
1 large onion, diced small
1 1/2 pounds white mushrooms, sliced
1 London broil, 3 to 3 1/2 pounds, about 1 inch thick, well chilled
Flour, any kind
1/2 cup dry sherry or mirin
1/2 cup soy or other non-dairy milk (rice, grain, oat, almond)
4 sprigs thyme, leaves only
1/3 cup Tofutti brand sour cream
Good pinch nutmeg
Freshly ground pepper to taste

Heat 2 tablespoons of the oil and sauté the onions until translucent. Add the mushrooms and sauté until all liquids evaporate. Remove the sautéed mixture and reserve. Slice the meat very thin. Put the flour in a plate. Heat the remaining 2 tablespoons oil in the same skillet. Dredge the meat slices in the flour, shaking off the excess, and sauté briefly, about one minute on each side. Add the reserved mushroom mixture, sherry, milk, and thyme to the skillet and bring to a boil. Reduce the flame to medium and cook, covered, about 10 minutes. Gently stir in the sour cream, nutmeg, and pepper and heat through, not letting it come to a boil again so it does not curdle. Serve hot with noodles, rice, or mashed potatoes.

LAMB MOUSSAKA

I have streamlined this time-consuming dish by roasting the eggplant, making the dish much lighter to boot. Watch how fast it will disappear! Nothing beats a good lamb dish, and there's no need to buy an expensive cut here; ground lamb is quite affordable. You can now enjoy the dairy-free version of the classic, and share it with a crowd. It tastes even better the next day. For a more dramatic presentation, choose 8 small eggplants, prepare the eggplant and the sauce as instructed, and assemble small individual moussakas, layering them in the order given.

Makes 10 ample servings

4 large eggplants, sliced lengthwise 1/3 inch
Vegetable spray
1/3 cup olive oil
2 large onions, quartered
12 large garlic cloves
1 large bunch flat parsley
1 large bunch mint, leaves only
1 small bunch cilantro, tough stems discarded
3 pounds lean ground lamb
3 cups crushed tomatoes
2 tablespoons curry
1 teaspoon turmeric
2 teaspoons allspice
2 teaspoons cinnamon
Ground pepper to taste
1 cup Tofutti brand sour cream

Preheat oven to 450 °F.

Line 2 cookie sheets with foil. Spray heavily with vegetable spray. Place the eggplant slices and spray heavily again. Bake 20 minutes, or a little longer, until nicely brown. Transfer the eggplant to a tray and set aside. Reduce the oven temperature to 350 °F.

Meanwhile, make the filling: Heat the oil in a large heavy skillet. In a food processor, coarsely grind the onion, garlic, parsley, mint, and cilantro. Add the ground mixture to the oil, and sauté 2–3 minutes. Add the lamb and cook 2–3 more minutes, breaking up the lamb as you go to make sure it gets evenly browned. Add the remaining ingredients and cook 2–3 more minutes.

Assemble: Spray a 9×13-inch lasagna pan with vegetable spray. Cover with a layer of eggplant (use a third of the slices). Top with half the filling. Top with another third of the slices. Top with the rest of the filling. Top with the remaining slices. Spray the whole top with vegetable spray. Bake 35 minutes. Let the dish rest about 10 minutes, then cut into squares. Serve hot.

Desserts

- 🍽 Cheesecake with strawberry sauce
- 🍽 Pecan streusel coffee cake
- 🍽 Tiramisu
- 🍽 Open face apple tart
- 🍽 Lemon coconut tart
- 🍽 Fruited Indian rice pudding
- 🍽 Crème caramel
- 🍽 Chestnut almond pudding with chocolate sauce
- 🍽 Pistachio halva mousse with maple sauce
- 🍽 Peanut butter chocolate bars
- 🍽 Chocolate truffles
- 🍽 Triple ginger cookies
- 🍽 Chocolate chip cookies
- 🍽 Ice cream
- 🍽 Praline chocolate log

DAIRY-FREE DESSERTS

I can make virtually any dessert delicious without using dairy products and without using junk products. I have long since stopped thinking of non-dairy ingredients as clever gimmicks to deflect attention from the absence of dairy products. Dairy-free desserts are a challenge I happily took on long ago—with fabulous results. Many people are at a loss about how to bake good non-dairy desserts because they imagine their hands will be totally tied. To put it bluntly, they don't believe it is possible to make delicious desserts without dairy products. I would feel the same way if all I knew about were those dreadful gooey plastic desserts one can buy for "convenience" (but not for enjoyment, let alone good health).

I am often reminded of a great line from a wheelchair-bound friend of mine (who, by the way, gets around magnificently). When I first met her, she said to me: "I never, ever dwell on what I *cannot* do. I only think of what I *can* do—and do it to the utmost." That's how I develop my dairy-free desserts. I simply go for broke. I explore and experiment with the most nondescript and homely yet most natural ingredients for texture, never using them for flavor, and let them do their magic. I make extensive lists of every imaginable baking product and end up with more wonderful items than I will ever need—nut butters and nut oils; premium chocolate products; pure extracts, flavorings, and liqueurs; sugar and other sweeteners; fruit juices; flours and thickeners; soy milk, rice milk, oat milk, almond milk, and coconut milk; soy cream cheese and sour cream; nuts and seeds; dried fruit. It's a long list, and everything on it is the best in caliber and quality.

In the late 1970s, when a few family members and I were running a bakery, we won an award for best carrot cake in the city. I remember our pioneer days, when we took our baked goods to Zabar's, Macy's, and dozens of restaurants around the city. (We didn't mind schlepping in those days when we were so young!) At fairs in Central Park and around the city, we prepared industrial quantities of carrot cake and chocolate cake, and we sliced till we dropped. Everyone raved about them, yet they were 100 percent non-dairy and natural. Now, those desserts define me as a cook. My kosher customers and my cooking class students constantly request them as a finale to meat meals, which preclude any dairy dessert. And my dairy-intolerant customers and students clamor for them because they want to have their cake and eat it too.

It doesn't happen much anymore, but I still occasionally hear people grumble that unless cookies have that wonderful butter flavor, they simply can't be good. To which I say: Is that so? Why not a wonderful chocolate flavor, or a coffee or rum flavor, or the flavor of orange flower water or of oatmeal? Cookies are a real showcase for me. Indeed, some of the cookies I make are not an indulgence, but are actually good for you. Sweetened naturally and packed with oats, raisins, seeds, and nuts, you could occasionally, as we do at home, forego lunch and enjoy half a dozen of these gems with coffee, without any guilt whatsoever.

Here's a story that I think will illustrate perfectly my perennial quest for the perfect flavor. My daughter-in-law Ruthie's father, Alex, shared this story with me as a way of thanking me for a party I catered for his company. An old Russian man was known in a tiny village for the wonderful tea he made. People came from far and wide to sample his tea. He adamantly refused to divulge the secret of his recipe, that is, until he became very ill and his children, seeing him slip away, dreaded losing that fabulous source of wealth along with their father. After much prompting and cajoling, he finally consented to share his secret. He gathered all his children around his deathbed, and, as they hung on his every word, he whispered: "Put in *a lot of tea*!" So that's it!

The secret of something good is to spread the good stuff thick, be it tea or any other flavor, as opposed to relying constantly on emulsions obtained with the heavy use of creams or eggs. It sounds infuriatingly simple. But that's what it's all about. I am not sorry to share that secret with everyone while I am alive and well, because I get my wish—getting people in the kitchen so they can develop a healthy, uncomplicated, fearless approach to food and cooking.

My mother—whom I credit for giving me an immense respect for raw materials and artisanal preparations, and a burning desire to get my hands on them and turn them into wonderful things to eat—always prepared ice cream with oil. Fantastic ice cream, I might add. I can see you shuddering. Gross, you probably think. But why? The oil is there only to ensure texture. I am not relying on it for any flavor, only for the perfect emulsion. Think of it as the culinary counterpart of hardware. Do you care if the hardware in your motor looks barbarous and impenetrable? After you slam the hood down, you will never see it. I make fabulous coffee, strawberry, chocolate, and praline ice cream, using a lot of, well, coffee, strawberries, chocolate, and praline—and only the best. These intense, bold, assertive flavors trump all others each time.

Of course, I readily agree that some ingredients are more lovable and inviting than others. Chocolate, coffee, strawberries? No problem! But what replaces the missing cream so essential to many delicious desserts? Well, let's take a simple example: tofu, a food that many people never even give a chance. And who can blame them? Let's just say that it wasn't love at first sight between me and tofu. The first time I spotted it at a supermarket, I exclaimed, what on earth is this pale, damp, jiggly, wobbly, rubbery slab doing in the produce section? Am I supposed to cook with it? Just how far were we supposed to take our culinary stoicism? "This is tofu," the supermarket salesman exclaimed with hurt pride. "Toe-*WHAT*?" I cried incredulously. But being a rebel, I bought some anyway and tried it, with great trepidation. It tasted awful. Undeterred, I decided to use it in a fruit mousse of some sort. I tossed it in the blender with some fresh berries. It tasted weird, but I sensed a vague promise and decided to prod on, experimenting with different proportions a dozen times. I soaked some dried apricots in warm water, mixed them with the tofu, sugar, orange peel, and apricot brandy, poured my mixture in stem glasses, chilled, and prayed. A couple hours later, I was met with the greatest kind of shock, the kind I wish on all of us: It tasted fabulous. Afraid to say a word about the alien to any of my guests, I served the fruit mousse for dessert, keeping my fingers crossed. I needn't have worried. My guests loved it and raved about it, but that commotion was nothing compared with the one that immediately followed after I spilled the beans. "What are you saying?" One of the guests said. "No cream? No butter?" Emboldened, I got into the habit of coaxing incredible treats from *the* blob. This was many years ago, long before it became the vogue to eat healthy (as if good health should be a passing fad!). Soy and other non-dairy products have none of the attributes that naturally attract us to food—color, fragrance, texture. But while rarely visible, they work their unseen magic in the finished dish—whether a mousse, a soup, a pie, or ice cream. No calorie problems, no meat conflicts, just some great liberation. Tofu, for one, has such a creamy texture and bulk that it needs little or no help from the usual suspects (mainly, cream and eggs) to achieve the smoothness we crave in ice cream, sauces, dips, lasagna, and so on. Bland and unobtrusive, it obediently highlights the flavors with which it is paired, giving them an incomparable texture that opens the door to many sweet and savory possibilities.

So, to conclude, just a little more missionary work and I will be done, promised. Only real flavors, please! There is no excuse for ersatz flavors (by the way, have you noticed that while they bear only a fleeting and offensive resemblance to their genuine counterparts, they cost exactly the same price?). Not artificial rum flavoring: **Rum!** Not imitation vanilla extract: **Vanilla extract!** Not cooking wine and cooking sherry: **Wine! Sherry!** Not chocolate-flavored drops: **Real chocolate chips!** An on and on, down the line. When you understand that, you are on your way. Beside the wonderful results you will get, your culinary "honesty" will deliver an immediate and long-lasting reward: You will be satisfied with less food, because you will have hit on the perfect flavor and will stop searching! I have a house full of thin and fit people to prove it.

CHEESECAKE WITH STRAWBERRY SAUCE

I love all my "babies," but this is one of my greatest triumphs. My daughter Bella recently asked me with great urgency whether I had thought of including this recipe in this book. "Whatever you do, don't forget this one!" she said, smacking her lips and patting her belly. Okay, so no, it is not dietetic food, but it is somewhat leaner and it is not laden with cholesterol as is its dairy counterpart. You will never want to go back to the dairy version. The strawberry sauce can be used with many other desserts (ice cream, pound cake, bread pudding, etc.)

Makes 16 servings

Crust

2 packages graham crackers (about 10 ounces total)
1/2 cup oil

Batter

4 containers Tofutti brand cream cheese
1 container Tofutti brand sour cream
1/3 cup lemon juice
1/4 cup cornstarch or arrowroot
1 1/4 cups sugar
4 eggs
1 tablespoon vanilla extract

Preheat oven to 375 °F.

Make the crust: In a food processor, grind the graham crackers and the oil to a fine powder. Press the ground mixture hard into the bottom of a 10-inch round spring form pan. Bake for 10 minutes. Remove the pan and reduce the temperature to 325 °F.

In a food processor or with an electric mixer, cream all the batter ingredients until smooth (not longer) and pour over the crust. Bake one hour and 10 minutes. Turn off the oven and leave the cake inside 2 more hours, without ever opening the oven. Take out and chill completely. Serve alone or with strawberry sauce (recipe follows).

Strawberry Sauce

1 12-ounce bag frozen unsweetened strawberries (or raspberries, strained to remove the seeds)
1 cup cranberry juice
1/4 cup crème de cassis (liquor stores)
1/4 cup fresh lemon juice
1 tablespoon corn starch (or potato starch, or arrowroot), mixed with a little water until dissolved

Bring all but last ingredient to a boil. Reduce the flame to low, add the corn starch mixture and cook, stirring, until just thickened and the mixture is no longer cloudy, about 1 minute. Puree in a blender or with an immersion blender until smooth. Cool completely before serving. Makes about 3 1/2 cups.

PECAN STREUSEL COFFEE CAKE

Perfect for breakfast, and so pretty with its layered look. Unlike its yeasted counterpart, it needs no kneading or rising and will keep well a couple of days, so go ahead and make it in advance if you need to; it will only get better.

Makes a dozen servings

Filling and Topping

3/4 cup firmly packed light brown sugar
1/4 cup all-purpose flour (or whole wheat *pastry* flour, or spelt)
2 tablespoons cold natural non-hydrogenated margarine (health-food stores)
3/4 cup pecans
1 1/2 tablespoons cinnamon

Cake

2 cups sifted all-purpose flour (or whole wheat *pastry* flour, or spelt)
1 teaspoon baking soda
1 teaspoon baking powder
Good pinch salt
1/2 cup natural non-hydrogenated margarine (health-food stores), at room temperature
1 cup sugar
3 eggs

1 cup Tofutti brand sour cream (or soy yogurt)

Preheat the oven to 350 °F

Make the filling-topping: Place all the filling ingredients in the food processor and pulse a few times, until the mixture resembles coarse meal. Transfer to a bowl and set aside.

Grease a 10-inch spring form pan and sprinkle very lightly with flour, tapping the bottom to shake out the excess. Mix the flour, baking soda, baking powder, and salt in a bowl. Cream the margarine and sugar with an electric mixer at high speed until light and fluffy. Beat in the eggs, one at a time, until light and fluffy. Add the flour mixture alternately with the sour cream to the batter, on low speed, beginning and ending with the flour mixture. Scrape half the batter into the prepared pan. Sprinkle evenly with half the filling. Pour the rest of the batter slowly and uniformly, making sure you don't disturb the first layers, and top with the remaining pecan mixture. Bake 35 to 40 minutes, or until the cake is golden and a knife inserted in the center comes out clean.

TIRAMISU

Italian for "pick-me-up," probably because it puts together three of our favorite intense, robust flavors: rum, chocolate, and coffee (please don't try to substitute any of them!). This dessert is so fabulous that I never bother to make the original dairy version. It's also healthier, thanks to my staunch ally tofu. When you serve it, don't tell anybody about the tofu until they have tasted and raved about it.

It is fine to use good store-bought sponge cake. Although sponge cake is not as pretty as ladyfingers, I prefer it because it maintains its shape better when soaked in the espresso and brandy. Lining the mold with plastic wrap allows very easy unmolding, just pull up the sides and the cake will lift right up. The chocolate must be only the best, as always! To chop chocolate, scrape the block vertically with a sharp knife: it will fall off in little shards or curls. Once you have all the ingredients in place, the dessert takes only a few minutes to assemble. Try your best to make this dessert a few hours before serving time, or even the day before, in order to give the dessert ample time to soak up all the flavors.

Makes 12 generous servings

1 1/4 pounds store-bought sponge cake
1 pound silken tofu, thoroughly drained and dried with layers of paper towels
2 tablespoons oil
1/2 cup sugar
1 container Tofutti brand cream cheese
2 1/2 tablespoons instant espresso powder, dissolved in 2/3 cup hot water
1/4 cup brandy, rum, or bourbon
8 ounces best quality semi-sweet chocolate, chopped

Preheat the oven to 375 °F.

Slice the sponge cake in half-inch thick pieces and toast in the oven for about 15 minutes, turning the slices over once, until medium-brown on all sides. Let cool.

In a food processor, process the tofu with the oil and sugar until perfectly smooth. Add the cream cheese, and process for a few more seconds. Pour the mixture into a bowl. Combine the coffee mixture and brandy in a container equipped with a spout, such as a glass measuring cup.

Grease a 2-quart (8 cup) loaf pan and line with plastic wrap, letting the sides overhang. Line the bottom completely with slices of cake, trimmed to fit tightly. Pour half of the coffee mixture evenly and carefully over the cake. Spread half of the tofu mixture evenly over the cake. Sprinkle half of the grated chocolate over the tofu mixture. Repeat: cake, coffee, tofu mixture, chocolate. Fold the overhanging plastic wrap toward the center of the mold. Refrigerate a few hours until set. Unmold and slice.

OPEN FACE APPLE TART

I have my mother to thank for providing the inspiration for this beautiful tart. The base is not a classic pie crust as we know it, more like a cookie dough, making this tart much less perishable than the classic apple pie. Apples and apricot jam are a wonderful match. You will create in no time a dessert that looks as professional as it tastes. Just be sure to get one of those fluted spring form pie plates, which make unmolding easy as, well, pie. This is a very good example of how elegant rustic can be.

Makes 8 to 10 servings

Dough

2 cups all-purpose flour
1 1/2 teaspoons baking powder
2 eggs
2/3 cup orange juice
1 teaspoon vanilla extract
2/3 cup sugar
1/2 cup oil
1 tablespoon grated lemon zest

4 Granny Smith apples, unpeeled, quartered and cut in thick wedges

Glaze

1/2 cup apricot jam
2 tablespoons lemon juice
2 tablespoons brandy

Preheat the oven to 375 °F.

Mix all the dough ingredients by hand or in a food processor, processing very minimally, pulsing just 2–3 times, until just combined. The mixture will look loose. Pour uniformly into a large (11–12 inch) round spring form pie plate, or 2 rectangle strip spring form molds. Stand the apple wedges in the dough, close together, pointed sides down, leaving a half-inch rim all around. Bake 30 to 40 minutes, or a little longer, until the dough and apples look golden brown.

Make the glaze: Mix the jam, lemon juice, and brandy in a food processor until perfectly smooth. Brush the glaze evenly on the tart while it is still hot, using it all up. Serve warm or at room temperature.

PLUM TART

Make the exact same dough, using pomegranate or cranberry juice instead of orange juice. Substitute 8 to 10 ripe black plums for the apples, proceeding exactly as for the apple pie. Sprinkle 1/2 cup sugar all over the plums before baking. No glaze.

LEMON COCONUT TART

Another wonderful treat I created with the help of tapioca flour. And how can I miss, pairing lemon and coconut? You will love to make this tart, because you can bake the crust fully and make the filling two to three days ahead of time, and assemble it on party day. Topping it with toasted coconut intensifies the coconut flavor and gives it a dramatic presentation. Have you noticed that coconut lovers cannot believe there is anyone out there who is not crazy about coconut?

Makes a dozen ample servings

Pie Dough

1/2 cup natural non-hydrogenated margarine (health-food stores), at room temperature
1/2 cup sugar
Pinch salt
2 eggs
2 teaspoons vanilla extract
1 tablespoon lemon zest
2 cups flour

Lemon Coconut Filling

2/3 cup sugar
1/3 cup tapioca flour
Pinch salt
2 tablespoons lemon zest
1/2 cup fresh lemon juice, strained
3 tablespoons rum or brandy
2 eggs
1 15-ounce can coconut milk
1 1/2 cups sweetened grated coconut

1/2 cup sweetened grated coconut, toasted about 12 minutes in a 300 °F oven

Preheat the oven to 350 °F.

Make the pie shell: With an electric mixer, cream the margarine, sugar, and salt until light. Add eggs one at a time and cream until light and fluffy. Add the vanilla extract, zest, and flour and mix just a few more seconds. Spread the dough uniformly in an 11-inch spring form pan, coming up the sides. Crimp the edges all around with 2 fingers. Pierce the bottom all over with a fork. Bake 40 minutes or until golden brown. Let the crust cool completely.

Make the filling: Put a small pot of water on to boil. Reduce the heat to low, and keep the water at a simmer. Place a bowl on top of the water, and put in the sugar, tapioca, salt, zest, lemon juice, and rum, whisking (beating with an electric mixer will work very well, too). When hot, add the eggs, whisking constantly until thick. Add the coconut milk and whisk only until the mixture looks smooth. Take the bowl off the double boiler, and stir in the coconut. Let the mixture cool completely, and pour into the baked crust. Chill. Sprinkle with the toasted coconut just before serving.

FRUITED INDIAN RICE PUDDING

Lest you think rice pudding is too much of a comfort food to be offered to serious grownup company, I have jazzed it up with a little Indian inspiration. Here is my own version, ready in no time and much less sweet and cloying than the Indian native, and good for you. Go for it!

Makes 8 servings

3/4 cup rice flour
1/4 cup tapioca flour
4 cups soy or other non-dairy milk (rice, grain, oat, almond)
4 cups coconut milk (light okay, but regular will be richer and creamier)
1/2 cup maple syrup
1/2 cup chopped pistachios
1/2 cup golden raisins
Grated peel of one orange
2 tablespoons orange flower water (specialty food stores)
2 good pinches saffron
1 tablespoon cardamom
Good pinch salt

In a heavy non-reactive pot, whisk the rice and tapioca flours in some of the milk until smooth. Turn on the heat and add all the remaining ingredients. Bring to a boil, whisking occasionally. Reduce the flame to low, and cook, covered, 20 minutes. Let the mixture cool to room temperature. Serve alone or with a scoop of coconut sorbet.

CRÉME CARAMEL

We grew up with this very unpretentious and delightful dessert, which my mother used to whip up on lazy Sunday afternoons. Caramel, eggs, and milk are practically all it takes. I add non-dairy milk powder and a little oil to augment the milk fats in the dish. The trick with this dish and all egg-based dishes is to bake it until just barely set, as further heating will toughen the custard.

Makes about 10 servings

Caramel

3/4 cup sugar
1/4 cup water

Batter

4 cups whole soy or other non-dairy milk (rice, oat, grain, almond), heated to just below boiling
1 cup soy or rice milk powder
1/4 cup vegetable oil
1/4 cup white corn syrup
1/4 cup sugar
2 tablespoons vanilla extract
8 eggs

Preheat the oven to 350 °F.

Make the caramel: Heat the sugar and water on a medium-low flame in a small saucepan, undisturbed, for about 5 minutes. It will turn a deep amber brown. Immediately turn off the heat (as sugar could go from just done to burned in no time) and very carefully pour into a round ring mold or 8 ramekins. Quickly swirl the sugar in the molds to let it cover the bottoms and come about half an inch up the sides.

Make the batter: Place all ingredients in a blender and blend until completely smooth (or place all the ingredients in a glass bowl and use an immersion blender). Pour the mixture into the mold or ramekins. Place the mold or ramekins in a baking pan containing just enough hot water to come up one third of the height of the molds. Bake about 40 minutes. Let the dessert cool. Unmold by loosening the sides with a knife, then put a rimmed dish slightly larger than the mold against the opening and flip onto the dish. The caramel will arrange itself beautifully around the custard.

VARIATIONS

Lemon crème caramel: Reduce the milk to 3 1/2 cups and add 1/2 cup lemon juice and 2 tablespoons fresh lemon zest.
Coffee crème caramel: Add 2 tablespoons instant coffee powder to the batter and 3 tablespoons rum or brandy.
Chocolate crème caramel: add 1/4 cup cocoa powder and 1/3 cup semisweet real chocolate chips to the milk while it is still very warm to dissolve them completely.

CHESTNUT ALMOND PUDDING WITH CHOCOLATE SAUCE

I almost never bother with fresh chestnuts, even though I love them, because of all the fuss they demand. Dry chestnuts are available year round and work beautifully. So, here is one of my latest matches: chestnuts, almonds, chocolate—it doesn't get better than that. This dessert is healthy, easy, and quick yet elegant. The chocolate sauce is wonderful with cakes, puddings, or to dip strawberries or orange slices in.

Makes 10 servings

3 cups soy or other non-dairy milk (rice, grain, oat, almond)
1 cup dry chestnuts (health food stores)
2 tablespoons agar-agar flakes or powder (health food stores)
1 cup soy or other non-dairy milk
1 1/2 cups unblanched almonds, ground fine in a food processor
3/4 cup maple syrup
2 tablespoons orange flower water (health food stores)
Good pinch salt
1 pound silken tofu, drained

In a saucepan, bring the 3 cups milk and chestnuts to boil. Reduce the heat to medium-low and cook, covered, 30 minutes. Mix the agar-agar with the cup of milk and let it sit a minute or two. Add the agar mixture, almonds, maple syrup, orange flower water, and salt, and cook 10 more minutes. Transfer the mixture to a food processor. Add the tofu and cream until perfectly smooth. Transfer to a mold, or to small bowls or glasses, and chill. Serve alone or with chocolate sauce.

Chocolate Sauce

Makes about 3 cups

1 cup soy or other non-dairy milk (rice, grain, oat, almond)
1/4 cup soy milk or rice milk powder
1/4 cup corn syrup, light or dark
1 teaspoon instant coffee powder
1 1/2 cups semisweet real chocolate chips
1/4 cup natural non-hydrogenated margarine (health-food stores), at room temperature
Pinch salt

In a heavy saucepan, whisk the milk and milk powder until smooth. Turn on the heat, add the corn syrup and coffee, whisking until hot but not boiling. Reduce the heat to low, and add the chocolate chips, whisking until smooth. Turn off the heat and add the margarine and salt, whisking until smooth and glossy. The sauce will thicken as it cools. Microwave very briefly it if has thickened too much.

CHOCOLATE

You will be amazed at the difference between desserts made with an institutional or mediocre brand and those made with a premium brand. My favorite line of chocolate products is Callebaut, because most of the items are kosher and non-dairy, and because it is fabulous and affordable.
In the absence of a good brand name (Callebaut, Ghirardelli, Droste, Hershey's, etc.) then read labels carefully: pure cocoa powder, real chocolate chips, real chocolate, etc.

PISTACHIO HALVA MOUSSE WITH MAPLE SAUCE

If you are a halva lover, this is for you. Yum! It is decadently rich, but a little serving of it is all you need to assuage your craving. It takes minutes to make and only a couple hours to set. You will love the maple sauce, with this and other desserts: over ice cream, with bread pudding, cheesecake, or crepes, to name a few.

Makes 12 small servings

1 1/2 cups soy or other non-dairy milk (rice, grain, oat, almond)
1/3 cup soy or rice milk powder
1/4 cup tapioca flour
1 1/4 pounds vanilla halva, crumbled
1 pound silken tofu, drained thoroughly
1/2 cup tehina paste
2/3 cup pistachios, coarsely ground and toasted 10 minutes in a 325 ºF oven

Place the milk, milk powder, and tapioca flour in a small saucepan, and whisk until smooth. Turn on the heat and cook on a very low flame, whisking, until the mixture is thick and smooth and comes to just below boiling. Transfer the mixture to a food processor, add the halva, tofu, and tehina, and process until perfectly smooth. Fold in the pistachios with a spoon. Pour into a greased loaf pan lined with plastic, or 12 greased small ramekins and freeze. Take the dessert out of the freezer a few minutes before serving, so it is easier to serve and eat. Serve alone or with maple sauce (below).

Maple Sauce

Makes about 1 3/4 cups

1/2 cup pure maple syrup
1/4 cup dark corn syrup
1/4 cup soy or rice milk powder
1/2 cup soy or other non-dairy milk (rice, grain, oat, almond)
1/4 cup dark rum

Whisk all the ingredients in a small saucepan until smooth. Turn on the heat to medium-low and cook for about 5 minutes. Let the sauce cool completely before storing in a glass jar in the refrigerator.

PEANUT BUTTER CHOCOLATE BARS

I created these to celebrate the discovery that my granddaughter was no longer allergic to peanut butter, and since she has a chocolate obsession, this was the ultimate gift. To get into her heart even faster, I threw in some Rice Krispies. We were buddies even before then, but afterwards . . . well, here I am, giving out all the secrets of my popularity with kids, big and small! (Maybe the drop of rum included in each bar helps too?) There is no party at my house without these bars. Because they keep so well, I would hate to see you divide the recipe. As always, use only the best chocolate! You can substitute almond or hazelnut butter, but whatever nut butter you use, read the ingredient list, and make sure it lists roasted nuts, not raw, so as not to lose that extra layer of flavor. After you add in the Rice Krispies, it will feel, for just a minute or two, like you are mixing mortar, but I assure you, it tastes infinitely better!

Makes about 80 bars

1 1/2 cups corn syrup, light or dark
2 cups smooth peanut butter
1 cup sugar
1 cup pure cocoa powder
1/4 cup instant coffee powder, mixed with 1/4 cup warm water
1/2 cup rum

10 cups Rice Krispies

3 cups semisweet real chocolate chips
2 tablespoons oil

Place the corn syrup, peanut butter, sugar, cocoa, coffee mixture, and rum in a large pot, and heat on a low flame until the mixture is smooth (this will take about 5 minutes). Add the Rice Krispies and combine thoroughly, still on the flame, with a wooden spoon. Pour the mixture while still warm onto a large, well-greased 1-inch deep cookie sheet. Pat the mixture very firmly and uniformly. Refrigerate until firm, about 1 hour.

Melt the chocolate chips with the oil 2 minutes in the microwave, or on a very low flame. Mix with a spoon until smooth, and spread evenly on the cooled mixture (an offset spatula would be the best tool for this step). Cool again about 1 hour. Using a sharp knife, cut into bars 1 inch wide and 2 inches long. Store refrigerated in an airtight tin.

CHOCOLATE TRUFFLES

After sharing this recipe and all its variations with you, I am sure that all of you chocolate lovers will think of me very kindly. For the ultimate gift, multiply this recipe, then divide in 2–3 equal parts and add a different flavor to each. I wish you this kind of danger everyday! They look as professional and taste as delicious as if you had bought them in the best boutique. A guest recently caused total consternation at my dinner table when he declared he didn't care for chocolate. A chocolate-addict friend of mine seated near him looked at him in horror, as if he had admitted to being a criminal of some sort, and proceeded to ignore him the rest of the meal. Fortunately for him, the evening was just winding down! Could it be he had just never tasted good chocolate before?

Makes a dozen truffles

1/2 cup soy or rice milk powder
1/2 cup soy or other non-dairy milk (oat, rice, grain, almond)
1/2 cup natural non-hydrogenated margarine (health-food stores)
2 cups semisweet real chocolate chips
1/4 cup pure cocoa powder
1/2 cup confectioner's sugar
1 egg yolk
1/4 cup brandy, rum, or bourbon

Whisk the milk powder and the milk in a small saucepan until smooth. Turn on the heat, set at a low flame, and add the margarine, chocolate chips, cocoa powder, and sugar. Whisk until the mixture is just melted. Turn off the heat, add the egg yolk and brandy, and mix until incorporated. Refrigerate the mixture until set, a couple hours. Shape into little balls (do not smooth: leave them a little bumpy; that is the trademark of truffles), and roll into cocoa powder. Keep refrigerated and tightly covered in plastic wrap until serving.

VARIATIONS

- Coffee truffles: Add 1 tablespoon instant coffee.
- Peppermint truffles: Omit the rum, and add a few drops peppermint extract.
- Nut truffles: Add 1/2 cup coarsely chopped toasted hazelnuts or pecans to the mixture. Or place a toasted hazelnut in the center of each truffle.
- Raspberry truffles: Omit the rum, and add 1/2 cup seedless raspberry jam and 3 tablespoons Creme de Cassis to the mixture.
- Peanut butter truffles: Replace the margarine with 1/2 cup smooth peanut butter.
- Roll the truffles in chocolate sauce or ground toasted nuts instead of cocoa powder.

TRIPLE GINGER COOKIES

For ginger lovers only! These heavenly, melt-in-your-mouth cookies are a real celebration of one of my favorite flavors: ginger. I spread it on really thick, using it in every shape and form. This recipe is very versatile, so I am including a few variations.

Makes about 40 cookies

1 cup natural non-hydrogenated margarine (health-food stores)
3/4 cup sugar
1 teaspoon vanilla extract
1 egg
1/4 cup soy or other non-dairy milk (rice, oat, grain, almond)
1 teaspoon baking powder
Pinch salt
2 cups flour, any flour
1 cup corn starch
2 tablespoons grated fresh ginger
2 tablespoons ground ginger
1/4 cup finely minced preserved ginger (health food stores and specialty food stores)

Cream the sugar and margarine on high speed with an electric mixer, until light and fluffy. Add the vanilla extract and egg and mix again until smooth. Add the remaining ingredients gradually and beat on very low speed until just combined.

Shape the dough into logs about 6 inches long, 2 inches in diameter. Wrap each roll tightly in plastic wrap and secure the ends with twist ties. Refrigerate a few hours (or freeze about 1 hour if you are pressed for time), until firm enough to handle.

Preheat the oven to 350 °F.

Take out the logs one at a time, unwrap, and place on a cutting board. Cut with a sharp knife into uniform 1/8 inch slices, even a little thinner if you can, placing each slice onto a foil-lined cookie sheet as you go, half an inch apart. Bake 20 minutes, or a little longer, until golden brown. Do not let them get darker. Cool completely before storing in an airtight tin, at room temperature.

VARIATIONS

Lemon cookies: Omit all ginger flavors. Substitute lemon juice for the milk and add 3 tablespoons grated lemon zest.
Pecan cardamom cookies: Omit all ginger flavors. Add 1 cup finely chopped pecans (or almonds, or hazelnuts) and 2 tablespoons ground cardamom.
Anise sesame cookies: Omit all ginger flavors. Add 1 cup sesame seeds and 3 tablespoons anise seeds

CHOCOLATE CHIP COOKIES

I can never make enough of these. A few years ago, I was involved with a few friends in a massive fund-raising project and made a million cookies (yes, a million, and then some!). You would think I would get tired of them. Absolutely not! They freeze well and also keep fresh for several weeks in a sealed container. Besides using high quality ingredients, the secret of good chocolate chip cookies is a soft and chewy texture, achieved by baking them only until they are just cooked. A good cookie sheet makes a difference too: the heavier the better, as it distributes the heat evenly and gradually.

Makes about 50 cookies

2 eggs
1/2 cup white sugar
1 cup dark brown sugar, packed
3/4 cup plus 2 tablespoons vegetable oil
1 tablespoon vanilla extract
2 1/2 cups all-purpose flour, or any flour
3/4 teaspoon powder
3/4 teaspoon baking soda
Good pinch salt
1 1/2 cups real semisweet chocolate chips, the smaller the better

Preheat the oven to 375 °F.

Cream the eggs and sugars with an electric mixer until light and fluffy. Add the oil and vanilla, and mix in thoroughly. Add the flour, baking powder, baking soda, and salt, and mix at low speed. Fold in the chips by hand. Drop the cookies in heaping teaspoonfuls onto a cookie sheet lined with foil, 1 inch apart.

If the baking tray is professional heavy gauge, bake for 10–11 minutes. If it is lighter, bake for 8–9 minutes. The cookies will firm up as they cool, so do not be tempted to bake them longer or they will harden. Bake only one tray at a time.

Store in tin boxes. Separate each layer of cookies with foil or wax paper so they don't stick together.

ICE CREAM

What do all food professionals have in common? They are quite dogged! This was a real tour de force for me. Developing this recipe was a labor of love, which took me months and countless batches and caused me endless frustration, but I am told it was all worth it! It was declared delicious by all my (willing) tasting victims, and much superior to their commercial counterparts. Just two pieces of advice: Buy yourself a 2-quart ice cream maker; and take the ice cream out of the freezer a few minutes before serving so it can reach the proper consistency. Remember, we are not manufacturers, and while we can make it delicious, we don't have all their tools at our disposal to make it the ideal texture without a little tweaking.

Makes 6–8 cups

Chocolate Ice Cream

2 cups soy or other non-dairy milk (rice, almond, oat, grain)
1/2 cup soy or rice milk powder
1/2 cup tapioca flour
1/2 teaspoon salt
2 cups soy milk
4 eggs
1/2 cup oil
1 cup sugar
1/2 cup light corn syrup
1 cup semisweet real chocolate chips
1/4 cup pure cocoa powder
1 tablespoon coffee powder, optional

In a bowl set over a saucepan of simmering water, using a hand mixer or an immersion blender, whip the 2 cups milk, milk powder, tapioca flour, and salt until smooth. Add the remaining milk and heat, beating, until very hot but not boiling. Add the eggs, oil, sugar, and corn syrup and whip 2 more minutes. Add the chocolate chips, cocoa, and coffee if using, and whip 1–2 more minutes, until the custard is thick enough to coat the back of a spoon. Chill the mixture completely. Transfer into a 2-quart ice cream maker and freeze following manufacturer's instructions.

Vanilla Ice Cream

2 cups soy or other non-dairy milk (rice, almond, oat, grain)
1/2 cup soy or rice milk powder
1/2 cup tapioca flour
1/2 teaspoon salt
2 cups soy milk
4 eggs
1/2 cup oil
1 cup sugar
1/2 cup light corn syrup
3 tablespoons vanilla extract (if you get more ambitious, use 1 vanilla bean, scraped, and strain the mixture)

In a bowl set over a saucepan of simmering water, using a hand mixer or an immersion blender, whip the 2 cups milk, milk powder, tapioca flour, and salt until smooth. Add the remaining milk and heat, beating, until very hot but not boiling. Add the eggs, oil, sugar, and corn syrup and whip 2 more minutes. Add the vanilla extract and whip just a few more seconds. Chill the mixture completely. Transfer into a 2-quart ice cream maker and freeze following manufacturer's instructions.

Strawberry Ice Cream

1 1/4 cups soy or other non-dairy milk (rice, almond, oat, grain)
1/2 cup soy or rice milk powder
1/3 cup tapioca flour
1/2 teaspoon salt
1 1/2 cups pomegranate or cranberry juice
4 eggs
1/2 cup oil
2/3 cup sugar
1/2 cup light corn syrup
1/4 cup fresh lemon juice
3 tablespoons crème de cassis (optional, but wonderful)
5 cups frozen unsweetened strawberries, puréed

(Continued on page 110)

In a bowl set over a saucepan of simmering water, using a hand mixer or an immersion blender, whip the milk, milk powder, tapioca flour and salt until smooth. Add the juice and heat, beating, until very hot but not boiling. Add the eggs, oil, sugar, corn syrup, and lemon juice and whip 2 more minutes. Add the liqueur and strawberries and whip just a few more seconds. Chill the mixture completely. Transfer into a 2-quart ice cream maker and freeze following manufacturer's instructions.

ADDITIONS

Rum raisin: Vanilla recipe. Fold in 1/4 cup rum and 3/4 cup raisins just before freezing.

Praline or roasted nuts: Vanilla recipe, or chocolate recipe. Fold in 1 cup praline powder (pp) or 3/4 cup coarsely chopped roasted nuts just before freezing.

Maple pecan: Vanilla recipe. Substitute 1 cup maple syrup for the sugar. Fold in 3/4 cup toasted pecans.

Chocolate mint: Chocolate recipe. Add a few drops peppermint oil.

Coffee: Vanilla recipe. Add 1/4 cup instant espresso powder to the custard, and add (optional) 1/4 cup rum or brandy just before freezing.

PRALINE CHOCOLATE LOG

I couldn't let go of this dessert section without including this giant "mother" party cake recipe. It is a stunning cake and tastes absolutely delicious. It is also much leaner, much less egg-y, much less sugar-y and contains much less fat than its traditional classic counterpart, making it more "affordable." Each component of this cake can be made quickly and separately a few days in advance and assembled in just a few minutes on serving day, up to a few hours before serving time. And finally and most importantly, each component is a valuable building block and can be used separately or together in a myriad of recipes, some of which I include here. The name of each part may not sound very orthodox to the pastry purists, but I hope to be forgiven after just two or three bites—and the next day when you discover you have no sugar or fat hangover. I always remember with pleasure a thank-you note I received from a customer after I prepared this cake for her wedding: "Dear Levana, you are the only caterer I know with a heart!"

Makes 20 ample servings

Nut Cake

1 cup hazelnuts
1/4 cup sugar
5 egg whites
Pinch salt
Pinch cream of tartar
3/4 cup sugar
1/4 cup cornstarch or arrowroot (Passover: potato starch)
5 egg yolks

To make the cake: Preheat the oven to 350 degrees.

In a food processor, grind the nuts with the sugar until fine. Set aside.
With an electric mixer set on high speed, beat the egg whites in a bowl with the salt and the cream of tartar until stiff. Add the sugar gradually and beat until very stiff. Add the cornstarch and beat 1 more minute. Reduce the speed to the lowest setting. Add the yolks and the nut mixture and beat until just incorporated, just a few seconds.

Pour the batter evenly onto a jellyroll pan lined with wax or parchment paper. Bake 15 minutes, or until the top springs back when touched lightly. Let the cake cool and cut across into 4 strips.

Coffee Buttercream

1/3 cup natural non-hydrogenated margarine (health-food stores), at room temperature
1/4 cup soy or other non-dairy milk (rice, oat, grain, almond)
1/2 cup brown sugar, packed
2 tablespoons instant coffee powder
1 1/2 cups confectioner's sugar

To make the buttercream: Heat all but last ingredient on a very low flame, or 1 minute in a microwave. With a whisk or an electric mixer, add the confectioner's sugar and beat until very smooth. Makes about 3 cups.

Chocolate Mousse

1 cup semisweet real chocolate chips, only the best
2 tablespoons instant coffee powder, decaf okay, mixed with 1/4 cup hot water
2/3 cup pure cocoa powder
2/3 cup sugar
1/4 cup vegetable oil
2 tablespoons brandy or rum
1 pound silken tofu, drained

To make the chocolate mousse: In a small saucepan, over a very low flame, melt the chocolate chips, coffee, cocoa, and sugar, mixing until just smooth (or microwave 2 minutes). Meanwhile mix the oil, brandy, and tofu in the food processor, and process a full minute. Add the chocolate mixture and process another minute, until perfectly smooth. Chill until firm. Makes about 4 cups.

Hazelnut Mousse

1 cup hazelnut butter
1 cup superfine sugar
1 pound extra firm tofu, drained and blotted dry with paper towels.

To make the hazelnut mousse: Place all the ingredients in a food processor, and process until perfectly smooth. Chill until firm. Makes about 3 1/2 cups.

Praline Powder

1 cup hazelnuts, toasted in a 350 degree oven for 15 minutes
3/4 cup sugar
1/4 cup water

To make the Praline Powder: Set the toasted nuts on an oiled, foil-lined cookie sheet and set aside.

Heat the sugar and water on a medium-low flame in a small saucepan for about 5 minutes, undisturbed. It will turn a deep amber brown. Immediately turn off the heat (sugar can go from just done to burned in no time). Quickly and uniformly pour over the nuts, and let the mixture cool completely, about 30 minutes. Break the mixture into chunks and place in a food processor. Grind into a medium-fine powder. Store in a glass jar. Makes about 2 cups.

Caramel Sauce

1 1/2 cups dark brown sugar, packed
1/4 cup dark corn syrup
1/3 cup water
3/4 cup soy or other non-dairy milk (rice, grain, oat, almond)
1/3 cup soy or rice milk powder
3 tablespoons brandy or rum
1 tablespoon vanilla extract

To make the caramel sauce: Bring the sugar, corn syrup, and water to boil in a small saucepan, stirring. Whisk the milk and milk powder in a little bowl until smooth. Carefully (to avoid splattering) add the milk mixture, brandy, and vanilla extract to the sugar mixture. Cook another 3 minutes on a medium flame, whisking until smooth. Let it cool completely before refrigerating. Makes about 2 1/2 cups.

To assemble: Line an oblong cake plate with plastic wrap, letting the sides overhang (it will be pulled out when the cake is all assembled so the platter stays clean). Place a layer of cake. Top with a 1/3-inch layer of chocolate mousse. Top with a layer of cake. Top with a 1/3-inch layer of hazelnut mousse. Top with a layer of cake. Mix the remaining hazelnut mousse with 3/4 cup praline powder, and spread on the cake 1/3-inch thick (you might have some mixture leftover). Top with a layer of cake. Spread the coffee buttercream on the top and the sides of the cake. The cake can be assembled several hours before serving. Gently pull out the plastic wrap from the bottom of the cake.

VARIATIONS

- The cake base can be made using any kind of nuts: walnuts, hazelnuts, almonds. Likewise, the praline powder can be made with any kind of nuts, and the hazelnut mousse can be made with any other kind of nut butter.
- The cake base can be a base for jelly rolls, or layered as it is here with other layers: simple syrup, liqueur, jam, whipped cream, chocolate sauce, etc.
- The praline powder is delicious as a topping on crème caramel, ice cream, or dessert sauces.
- Both the chocolate and hazelnut mousses are wonderful enough to be used each by itself or in combination, or as layers to a chocolate cake base, génoise, or jelly roll.
- Parfaits: Place the chocolate mousse in dessert glasses. Top with hazelnut mousse, sprinkle with praline powder.
- Caramel sauce: perfect over ice cream, bread pudding, pound cake, and roasted fruit.

Dips and Spreads

- 🍽 **Curried spinach dip**
- 🍽 **Red pepper butter**
- 🍽 **Green goddess sauce**
- 🍽 **Buttermilk dill dressing**
- 🍽 **Smoked salmon spread**
- 🍽 **Horseradish sauce**
- 🍽 **Thai dipping sauce**
- 🍽 **Herb cheese dip**
- 🍽 **Spicy tofu dressing**

The following dips and spreads are all a snap to make, and much lighter than their dairy counterparts. They all keep a good few days, and having them on hand will enhance many dishes and make them quite exciting. They work with salads, crudités, crackers, wraps, poached chicken or fish, to name a few.

CURRIED SPINACH DIP

Makes 2 1/2 cups

1 10-ounce box frozen chopped spinach, squeezed thoroughly dry
1 cup soy yogurt
1/2 pound silken tofu
1/2 cup Tofutti brand cream cheese
2–3 tablespoons curry powder
Salt and pepper to taste

Place all ingredients in a food processor and process until perfectly smooth.

RED PEPPER BUTTER

Makes about 2 cups

4 bottled roasted red peppers, blotted dry with paper towels
1 cup natural non-hydrogenated margarine (health-food stores)
2 tablespoons green peppercorns in brine, drained
1 tablespoon paprika
Salt to taste

Place all ingredients in a food processor and process until perfectly smooth.

GREEN GODDESS SAUCE

Makes about 2 1/2 cups

1 small bunch flat parsley

1 bunch watercress, stems and all
3 tablespoons capers
3 cloves garlic
Salt and pepper to taste
1 cup soy yogurt
1/2 cup Tofutti brand sour cream
1/4 cup Dijon mustard.

Blanch parsley and watercress just a few seconds in boiling water. Rinse under running cold water and squeeze thoroughly dry. Transfer to a food processor with all the remaining ingredients and blend until smooth.

BUTTERMILK DILL DRESSING

Makes about 2 1/2 cups

1 cup soy milk
1 tablespoon lemon juice or vinegar
1 small bunch dill, fronds and stems
1/3 cup olive oil
1 medium cucumber, peeled and seeded
1/4 cup fresh lemon juice
2 tablespoons sugar
Salt and pepper to taste

Mix the soy milk and lemon juice in a bowl. The mixture will curdle. Place the mixture in a food processor, with all the remaining ingredients, and blend until smooth.

SMOKED SALMON SPREAD

Makes about 1 1/2 cups

4 ounces smoked salmon
1 cup Tofutti brand cream cheese
Juice and rind of 1 lemon
8 sprigs dill, fronds and stems
4 scallions

Place all ingredients in a food processor and process until perfectly smooth.

HORSERADISH SAUCE

Makes about 2 cups

1/2 cup prepared white horseradish
1/2 pound silken tofu
1/2 cup soy or other non-dairy milk (rice, grain, oat, almond)
1/2 cup low fat mayonnaise
Salt and pepper to taste
3 tablespoons chopped chives

Place all but last ingredient in a food processor and process until smooth. Stir in the chives.

THAI DIPPING SAUCE

Makes about 2 cups

1 2-inch piece fresh ginger, peeled
1 stalk lemongrass, cut in large sections (skip if you have trouble finding it)
1/2 cup strong Lapsang Souchong tea (settle for Earl Grey)
1/2 cup coconut milk
1/2 cup peanut butter
1/4 cup soy sauce
1/4 cup rice vinegar
Good pinch cayenne

4 scallions, sliced thin
3 tablespoons minced cilantro

Grind the ginger and lemongrass in a food processor. Add all remaining ingredients, and process until perfectly smooth. Transfer to a bowl, and stir in the scallions and cilantro.

HERB CHEESE DIP

Makes about 2 1/2 cups

1 cup crumbled VeganRella cheddar flavor cheese
1/2 cup Tofutti brand cream cheese
1 cup soy yogurt
1/4 cup dry sherry or mirin
2 tablespoons *Herbes de Provence*

Place all ingredients in a food processor and process until perfectly smooth.

SPICY TOFU DRESSING

Makes about 2 1/2 cups

1 pound soft tofu, squeezed dry
4 large cloves garlic
1/4 cup olive oil
1/4 cup Dijon mustard
1/2 cup orange juice
1/3 cup wine vinegar
1 tablespoon oregano
Salt and pepper to taste

Blend tofu, garlic, and olive oil in a blender or food processor. Add all remaining ingredients and process until smooth.

A Few Favorite Drinks

- 🍽 Iced mocha
- 🍽 Hot chocolate
- 🍽 Pearl tea

A FEW FAVORITE DRINKS

I'll bet you thought specialty drinks were impossibly hard to make. Well, these are simple as anything, and they're fabulous. No store-bought counterparts come even close to homemade, especially the pearl tea, which I have greatly streamlined for you: yum! You guessed it: I don't serve soda at my house, unless asked nicely and repeatedly. I have a stash for those rare individuals who ask, and even they seem to ask less and less often. They are much happier when offered these concoctions.

ICED MOCHA

Makes 2 quarts

1/3 cup decaf or regular instant espresso powder, premium brand (Bustelo, Medaglia de Oro, etc.), a drop more if you like it stronger
1/2 cup hot water
1/4 cup premium brand chocolate syrup
2 cups soy or other non-dairy milk (rice, oat, grain, almond), or a little more if necessary to fill up the pitcher.

Dissolve the coffee in the water. Transfer the mixture to a 2-quart pitcher. Add the syrup and milk and stir. Add ice all the way to the top and stir thoroughly

HOT CHOCOLATE

Makes 6 servings

1/3 cup soy or rice milk powder
1 cup whole soy or other non-dairy milk (rice, oat, grain, almond)
2/3 cup semisweet real chocolate chips
1/4 cup cocoa powder
3 cups whole soy or other non-dairy milk (rice, oat, grain, almond)
1 tablespoon vanilla extract
2 tablespoons coffee powder, optional, if you want mocha

Pinch cayenne, optional

Place the soy milk powder with 1 cup soy milk in a saucepan, and whisk until smooth. Add all remaining ingredients and bring to just below boiling, whisking occasionally, until smooth and frothy. Serve hot.

PEARL TEA

Makes 6 servings

1/2 cup quick cooking tapioca (health food stores)
3 cups soy milk
2 teaspoons cinnamon
1/2 teaspoon ground cloves
2 teaspoons ground ginger
3 cups strong sweetened green tea, regular or decaf, chilled (any sweetener will be suitable)

Whisk the tapioca, milk, and spices in a saucepan until smooth. Turn on the heat and bring to a boil. Reduce to very low and simmer 3 minutes. Chill the mixture.

Pour the tapioca mixture into 6 glasses. Pour the cold tea over and mix. Serve cold.

> ### PEARL TEA VARIATIONS
>
> - Omit the spices, and use a flavored green tea: jasmine, lychee, mint, etc.
> - Serve hot.

CONVERSION CHART

The following conversions have been rounded up or down slightly to simplify measuring.

Weight	
American	Metric
1/4 oz	7 g
1/2 oz	15 g
1 oz	30 g
2 oz	60 g
3 oz	90 g
4 oz	115 g
5 oz	150 g
6 oz	175 g
7 oz	200 g
8 oz (1/2 lb)	225 g
9 oz	250 g
10 oz	300 g
11 oz	325 g
12 oz	350 g
13 oz	375 g
14 oz	400 g
15 oz	425 g
16 oz (1 lb)	450 g
1 1/2 lb	750 g
2 lb	900 g
2 1/4 lb	1 kg
3 lb	1.4 kg
4 lb	1.8 kg

Volume		
American	Metric	Imperial
1/4 t	1.2 ml	
1/2 t	2.5 ml	
1 t	5.0 ml	
1/2 T (1.5 t)	7.5 ml	
1 T (3 t)	15 ml	
1/4 cup (4 T)	60 ml	2 fl oz
1/3 cup (5 T)	75 ml	2 1/2 fl oz
1/2 cup (8 T)	125 ml	4 fl oz
2/3 cup (10 T)	150 ml	5 fl oz
3/4 cup (12 T)	175 ml	6 fl oz
1 cup (16 T)	250 ml	8 fl oz
1 1/4 cups	300 ml	10 fl oz (1/2 pt)
1 1/2 cups	350 ml	12 fl oz
2 cups (1 pint)	500 ml	16 fl oz
2 1/2 cups	625 ml	20 fl oz (1 pint)
1 quart	1 liter	32 fl oz

Oven Temperature		
F	Gas Mark	Description
225	1/4	Very cool/very slow
250	1/2	—
275	1	cool
300	2	—
325	3	very moderate
350	4	moderate
375	5	—
400	6	moderately hot
425	7	hot
450	8	—
475	9	very hot

ABOUT THE PHOTOGRAPHERS

MENACHEM ADELMAN, a commercial photographer since the late 1970s, operates a studio in the New York City area with his wife Leah. While mostly involved with assignments of traditional still life product images ranging from estate jewelry to food illustration, he also enjoys the opportunity to express artistic concepts with Jewish philosophical themes.

MEIR PLISKIN, young and talented Israeli-born assistant commercial photographer, specializes in nature and everyday scenes of the big city, and maintains a weblog to showcase his portfolio.

INDEX

RECIPE NOTES

_____

_____

_____

_____

_____

_____

_____